The Making of a Legacy

The Making of a Legacy

Bryson Brown

© 2012 by Bryson Brown. All rights reserved.

Published by Vantage Point Publishing
Indianapolis, IN 46218

No part of this publication may be reproduced or transmitted in any form or by any means, electronic or mechanical, including photocopy, or any information storage and retrieval system, without permission from the publisher. The only exception is a brief quotation in printed reviews.

Limit of Liability/Disclaimer of Warranty: While the publisher and author have used their best efforts in preparing this book, they make no representations or warranties with respect to the accuracy or completeness of the contents of this book and specifically disclaim any implied warranties of merchantability or facilities for a particular purpose. No warranty may be created or extended by any persons. The advice or strategies herein may not be suitable for your situation. You should consult with a professional where appropriate. Neither the publisher nor author should be liable for any loss of profit or any other incidental damages, including but not limited to special, consequential, or other damages.

This is a work of fiction. Names, characters, businesses, places, events and incidents are either the products of the author's imagination or used in a fictitious manner. Any resemblance to actual persons, living or dead, or actual events is purely coincidental.

ISBN 978-0-9883939-2-9

The publisher would appreciate notification where errors occur so that they may be corrected in subsequent printing and/or editions. Please send comments to the publisher by emailing to biz@amorousink.com

Printed in the United States of America

The Making of a Legacy

"A Poetic Journey through African American History from Chains to the White House"

Dedication

This book is dedicated to my late parents, Willie and Annie Brown. They laid the foundation for me to become the man that I am today. If it wasn't for their encouragement, guidance, love and support, this book could not have become a reality. If it wasn't for their mandate to read a book and to write a paper about that chosen book each week, I may have never discovered this love for reading and writing.

I would also like to dedicate this book to my late sister Brenda Brown-Bair. She was one of my inspirations for this book and she was the first person to tell me to write this book. She always told me to dream big and to chase my dreams.

Finally, I dedicate this book to my brother Zachary Warren, whose many talks and urging helped to bring life to this project.

No words that I could write could express how truly thankful I am that God blessed me with such loving parents, an awesome sister, and a supportive brother. You all will forever be with me and will always be missed.

Acknowledgments

First and foremost, I would like to thank my Heavenly Father, who loved the world so much that He gave the world His only begotten Son - my Lord and Savior Jesus Christ. I'm truly thankful for the gifts of expression and writing that God has blessed me with and for giving me the spiritual guidance to make this dream a reality. I could never have done this without the faith I have in You, the Almighty.

To my loving wife, Dr. Sharon Y. Brown: I can barely find the words to express my appreciation for all the love, support, and spiritual guidance, you've given me. I am so thankful for your editing skills. You are truly a blessing and I can't thank God enough for you. I love you and always will.

To my children, Dominique, Janelle, Gabrielle and Bryson, Jr.: If it wasn't for you this book may have never been written. Each of you deeply inspired the writing of this book. May this book be a symbol of my love for you and an inspiration for you to reach your full potential in life and be all that God has designed you to be!

To my sisters Loretta Canton and Cherry Lewis: I love you and cannot thank God enough for the best sisters in the world. Thank you for always believing in me. I would like to also thank my brothers-in-law Carl Canton and Bob Lewis for always treating me like their little brother.

To my family who I love dearly and I'm thankful for all of you for always encouraging and supporting me: Patricia Cole, Dorothy Brown, Charles and Joanna Pierce, Ralph and Sandra Finley, Charles and Alma Cole, Catherine Chase, nephews (Robert Darnell Lewis, Michael Canton, Craig Brown, Victor Bair, Andre Lewis, Christopher Bair, Jason Bair, Jonathan Finley, Benjamin Finley, Joshua Finley), nieces (Michelle

Brown, Trayce Wright, Rebeckah Finley, Jessica Martinez and Jasmine Pierce), godsons Davon Fountain and Tyler Williams and to all of my cousins who are far too many to mention, but are not forgotten in my heart. I love you all. A special thank you to the Bates family (Booker & Esther), Finnell family (Charles & Nora), McLamb Family (Larrie & Yvonne), and the Green/Summers family as well as Ms. Virginia Fountain who has always made me feel special. I would also like to thank my adopted Raleigh, NC families: the Haynes' (Leonard & Karen), Jones' (Garrick & Renee), Merritts (Sam & Tiffany), Rories (Reginald & Madonna), Smiths (Cassandra), Pam Bynem, Chapmans (Dean and Kim) and the Spencers (Jay & Karen).

To the Buckingham and Whiting families: I will always have a special place in my heart for you because of the love and support you gave to my mother and family.

To my brothers from other mothers, whether you're blood or not, God has blessed me with the best brothers in the world: Octavius Burnett, James Owens, Stefan Jordan, Raymond Bennett, Patrick McLamb, Booker Bates, Tobias "Truck" Walker, Brian Fountain, Charles Finnell, Jr., Troy Davis, Ralph Cato, Reginald Rorie, Clayton Brock, Leevance Williams, Ty Ward, Dwan Lee, John Williams, Patrick Kerr, Lester Walker, Pete Dorsey, Mack Appleberry, Garrick Jones, Tony House, Wesley Spencer, Michael Webb, Mark Robinson, Brian Hairston, Barry Martin, Kenny Bailey, Troy Ebron, Phil Myer, John Myer, Bruce Johnson, Calvin Hollman, Elombe Brathwaite, Bob Sterns, Keith Davidson, Harvey Lynch, Demarko Spriggs, Larry Pearson, Phil Brown, Destry Mangus, Brian Phoenix, Jamal Cromity, Matthew Foster, David Saunders, Jeffrey Lipscomb, Van Barrett, Steve Williams, Joe Williams, Rick Isom, Bill Braswell, Mark Kinnaird, Eric Mountain, John Bullock, Sterling Pettis, Michael R. Williams, Travis Totten, Phil Brickle, Todd Mungin, Lamont Morris, Arthur Robinson, Nathan Gadsden, Fred Hall, Kyle

Oliver, George Payne, Kirby Evans, and my little brother Keyon Sands.

To Dr. Richard Winchester: You were the best teacher/professor that I've ever had. Your knowledge of history and mentoring while at Lincoln University helped to make this book a reality.

To Dawn Rivers: Thank you for believing in this project and for your direction, expertise and guidance in making this book a reality.

To my dear friend Constance Fountain-Wormsley: You have been a great friend and I will always cherish our friendship. Thank you for all of the encouragement, support and many ideas over the years. I've been truly blessed to have a friend like you.

Thank you to the ladies whose encouragement and support have given me the confidence and motivation to finish what I started. You all have been on this journey with me offering advice, encouragement and support. I would like to again say thank you: Lisa Boulware, Aprile Cason, Judith Fitzgerald, Angela Greene, Delores Armstrong, Paulette Brock, June Spears, Nicole Foster, Dorothea Brock, Stacey Owens, Arleen Brooks, Melissa Morton, Geri Bushel, Kristine Daniels, Bernadette Davis, Teddi Scott-Felder (You know you should be on at least book three by now), Sandra Chambers, Deneen Hughes, Sonya Evans, Jewell Lester, Kim Moss, Darlene Mungin, Ruby Doub, Kelli Williams, Stephanie Harrison, Lesley Jordan-Anderson, Nancee Holley, Regina Crosby, Vernette Shaw, Yashica Woods-Buchanan, Pat Morton, Toria Williams, and Kelly Moore Walker.

I know I have forgotten someone so I apologize if I failed to mention your name. I still have much love for you.

To my Harrisburg, Pa; Raleigh, NC; Shaw University, Lincoln University, Penn State University, Brother to Brother Men's

Fellowship, and Phi Beta Sigma Fraternity, Inc families: Thank you for all of the love and support. I would also like to acknowledge my staff and co-workers at the Division of Health Service Regulation.

To my art contributors: I would like to say thank you to Aziiyza King, Sterling Pettis and Keyon Sands for their creativity, ideas and thoughts on helping to make this project complete. You all are truly awesome, gifted, and talented and may God continue to bless your gifts and talent.
And to my spoken word, poetry, and writers families: I would like to say thank you for given me the confidence to do this book: Leevance Williams - thank you for having my back. This couldn't have happened without you Bro. Julie Bush - your words of support mean more than you will ever know. Let's get that book started! Petrina Bryant - you are the queen of the microphone. Evelyn Katena Lemar- you truly are the Quiet Storm. Keisha Mark-Williams - you are seven and will always be my sister in poetry and an inspiration to me. Nathaniel Gadsden, Church Da Poet, Langston Fuze and Montrell Brooks – you all are the greatest.

Free Lamar Brown

As the caged bird sits behind the bars of a stolen future and sings his songs for freedom and justice, and is another victim of a broken justice system. A justice system that has promised justice for all and was designed for its courts to do what is right, but in the case of Lamar Brown has become an example of a travesty of justice. Become a voice for the falsely and wrongly convicted in America and allow justice to truly prevail.

TABLE OF CONTENTS

1. America Is Me
2. American History Is Not American History
3. From 1619 to Now
4. Imagine Being a Slave
5. They Were Born to Be Free - The Underground Railroad
6. A Well-Kept Secret
7. One Great Day - The Pennsylvania Grand Review
8. Robert Smalls Was an American Hero
9. I Am an African-American
10. Frederick Douglass
11. They Were Called the Buffalo Soldiers
12. The African-American Journey in America Tells a Story
13. Up from Slavery - Booker T. Washington
14. Reconstruction
15. The Wilmington Race Riot Was a Day of Blood and Terror
16. Lynching Is Also American History
17. America
18. What Is in a Name?
19. W. E. B. Du Bois Was a Voice
20. To Be Black Is Reason to Be Proud
21. The Flag
22. America Must Pay
23. How Did African-American History Become Irrelevant?
24. The Harlem Renaissance
25. Marcus Garvey - The Father of Black Nationalism
26. Black Ball - A League of Their Own

27. Her Name Was Mary McLeod Bethune
28. Charles Hamilton Houston Believed in America
29. Lloyd Gaines Was an American Mystery
30. Langston's Words
31. John Hope Franklin Believed in History
32. Joe Louis and Jesse Owens Were American Heroes
33. The Tuskegee Experiment - A Piece of History America Cannot Explain
34. Vivien Thomas Was a Man With a Dream
35. The Tuskegee Airmen Soared Like Eagles
36. America Should Know the Name Dorie Miller
37. The Few, the Proud, the Montford Point Marines
38. Dr. Benjamin Mays Wanted a Better America
39. Jackie Robinson - A Real American Hero
40. Henrietta Lacks Lives!
41. How Do You Name the Black Experience? (You Can't!)
42. Twenty-eight Days
43. Before There Was a Civil Rights Movement, There Was Vernon Johns
44. Sometimes You Only Need to Say the Name, Thurgood Marshall
45. One Name Truly Stands Out - Barbara Johns
46. A Day That Changed America Forever (Brown versus Board of Education of Topeka)
47. Medgar Evers and a New Day

48. Their Names Are Not Famous (The Little Rock Nine)
49. When I Think of the History of Black People in America
50. The Greensboro Four
51. Malcolm X
52. Taking a Stance Meant Taking a Seat
53. Dorothy I. Height - The Godmother of the Civil Rights Movement
54. The Civil Rights Movement Changed America
55. No Ordinary People
56. Forty-five Years, Nine Months and Thirteen Days
57. Float Like a Butterfly and Sting Like a Bee
58. Malcolm and Martin
59. Tommie Smith and John Carlos Made One Great Stance
60. Sometimes America Needs to Remember the Orangeburg Massacre
61. Martin Luther King, Jr. Had a Dream
62. Arthur Ashe
63. I Accept Your Apology, America
64. We Have Forgotten So Much
65. I Am an American
66. A Defining Day
67. Barack Obama
68. The Inheritance
69. Today Barack Obama is President
70. Let Us Not Forget to Vote!
71. January 15th
72. A Day to Remember (The Brown Decision under Attack)

73. Freedom Was Not Free
74. What Is American History?
75. A Look in the Mirror
76. One Month
77. Four More Years
78. I Am My Blackness

America Is Me

America is me
When I think about America
How could America not be me?
America stole me from my home
And enslaved my ancestors
Slavery in America!
Destroying families and culture
And for over 200 years
My people cultivated and developed America's land for free
America is me
Check out the history
My people helped make America free
Crispus Attucks was the first to die for America
And we have died in every war that America has fought in since
From the Revolutionary War to Iraq
How can America not be me?
Labeled three-fifths of a human
And stripped of all dignity
No name, No education and No rights
America is me
Declared to be free
But with no property or economic resources
Or any civil rights,
Nor laws to protect
Blacks in America were still not free
But still America is me
From free labor
To cheap labor
Blacks continued to build America
Share cropping
Industrializing of America
Working for almost free
America is me
Victimized, tortured, lynched and murdered

From slavery to Jim Crow
And discrimination and racism still exist
America is me
History books do not show
How America is me
American history does not always show the contribution that will show that America is me
My people helped to make America the land of the free
And without my people, where would America be?
America is me

American History Is Not American History

American history is not American history
If the history of African-Americans is told apart from American history and not as a part of African-American history
American history is not American history
If the history of African-Americans is not accurately told in the telling of America's story
American history is not American history
If the history of African-Americans is an afterthought in telling the story of the making of a nation
American history is not American history
If mere bits and pieces of the history of African-Americans is used in the curriculum to teach American history
American history is not American history
If contributions and facts are made to be distorted truths of American history
How can you teach the history of America!
And not tell the story of the African-American's journey in America?
How can you teach the history of America!
And not tell how African-Americans went from chains to the White House?
And how African-Americans helped to build a nation
How can you teach the history of America!
And not talk about the significant roles that African-Americans have played in what has made America the great nation that it is?
And how can you teach the history of America!
If America does not teach about that regrettable side of history that became a part of the African-American experience?
America is so ashamed of its past that a lot of history still remains unknown
The invisible history of the African-Americans

The echoes of America's past that America chooses to not often be reminded of
America's real legacy
America's version of true democracy
American history is not American history
When stories are left untold
When the contributions of so many remain unacknowledged
Historical act after historical act treated as if they never happened
And this is what we call American history?
A little bit of this and a little bit of that and a little bit of what is relevant
And that is the remembrance of America's past
Denied, disregarded and disrespected
And then to limit the contributions of African-Americans to a month long commemoration
The month of February, the shortest month of the year
Almost four hundred years of history condensed into twenty-eight days
Twenty-eight days is enough African-American history for America?
How can American history be American history!
When you have a systematic practice that neglects to touch on so much of American history?
African-American history is more than "I Have a Dream" and "We Shall Overcome"
African-American history is the contributions and strength of a people
And American history is not American history
If it does not tell the accurate and complete history and journey of all Americans

From 1619 to Now

From 1619 to now
From slavery to freedom
African-Americans have played a strong role in the making of America's history
A history of great accomplishments
A history of many contributions
But also a history of an oppressed people
And of great struggles and tragedies
From 1619 to now
Going from people of a dark continent
To Negro
To Colored
To Black
To African-American
And let us not forget Nigger
To what is next?
African-Americans have been a part of America
And America has helped define the African-American
African-Americans with their culture, history and legacy being stolen
But still through their journey
Have ensured their place in America's history
And even though it has not been fully recognized
The African-American's place in America's history cannot be denied
The African-American has built America
Cultivated America
Created for America
Fought for America
And has died for America
The African-American has helped to make America what it is today
From 1619 to now
Follow the journey

From the ordinary to the extraordinary
The African-American's history
Is who we are and what we are
Like it or not
The African-American's role in America's history has to be recognized
African-Americans are America's past
African-Americans are America's present
And African-Americans will be a part of America's future
From 1619 to now
From chains to the White House
African-Americans have played a strong role in the making of America's history
A fact that cannot be denied
American history
Some of the journey known
Some of the journey unknown
But still American history
A proud history
From 1619 to now

Imagine Being a Slave

Imagine being a victim of the greatest holocaust ever
Being captured or kidnapped by foreign invaders
Stolen to be sold
Taken away from your family and home
Imagine being stored in stockades like cattle
Waiting to be put on slave ships to take you to a place unknown
Never to see your family, home, or country again
Imagine being treated as cargo and merchandise
And being one of the countless millions of victims of the Trans-Atlantic Slave Trade
Imagine traveling what was known as the Middle Passage
Through some of the worst traveling routes and foul weather
And with such deplorable conditions on the slave ships, not even the worst criminals should ever have to endure
Imagine being stored in the lower decks of the slave ships in unsanitary conditions
Chained and packed on top of each other like sardines in a can
Forced to eat very little food which was usually spoiled and to drink contaminated water
On a journey that could last up to six months
Imagine having to smell the most awful stench imaginable
Watching others suffer from these terrible conditions
And being forced to watch many of your fellow captives die from disease, starvation and suicide
Struggling to hold onto your sanity and to understand why you are going through this hopeless plight
Imagine surviving the voyage and realizing your nightmare is not over
Forced to masquerade on a platform as potential buyers examine your body for purchase
Being sold to the highest bidder to work as a slave for the rest of your life
Taken to a plantation to become free labor

Imagine working long hours in the fields and in the home of the slave owner
Being a slave in America - the land of the free
But realizing that you are not free, but that you are a slave
Being forced to build a country that is not your own
Imagine cultivating the land and building the cities of America
Picking cotton, rice, sugar, and tobacco
Making the slave owners wealthy and America the wealthiest nation in the world
Imagine being broken of your spirit and made to feel inferior
Being powerless and having no control over your life
And having to come to the realization that you are a slave
And that you will probably be a slave for the rest of your life
Imagine being given a new name by the slave owner that purchased you as his property
Imagine having your family being sold and taken away from you
Imagine being branded and whipped to control and intimidate you
Imagine being labeled as less than a human being
Imagine having no civil or human rights or not being allowed to be educated
Imagine not being free
Imagine would it would be like being a slave

They Were Born to Be Free – The Underground Railroad

They were born to be free
Most slaves had the undying dream of one day being free
But for some slaves, the thought of being property for life was unthinkable
And as word traveled there was freedom and that this freedom was real
The determination to reach freedom was born in the minds of many slaves
They heard the journey to freedom was on the Underground Railroad
A network of people who helped fugitive slaves escape the horrors of plantation life
And were sympathetic to the cause of freedom for slaves
They heard this Underground Railroad would take them to the land of the free
Even though America was supposed to be the land of the free
For them America was a nightmare called slavery
And as the call for freedom was disseminated through word of mouth and songs
They listened for the codes and the messages in the words
They knew songs such as "Go Down Moses" and "Steal Away"
Offered the opportunity for the chance to be free
Their thirst for freedom gave them the courage to risk their lives
And to risk the possibility of capture and punishment
They knew they were leaving family and friends
And there was a chance they would never see them again
But the more they heard of freedom, the more they desired it
They knew God created them to be free, but man made them slaves
They knew they were not born to be the property of another human being
They knew they had to have freedom

They knew of the dangers of this passage to freedom during their unknown journey
But they also knew they had to face these dangers and risks to escape their bondage
And the unjust and cruel system of American slavery
They knew when the sound of freedom called
They were going to answer and they were going to follow those tracks to freedom
They were going to follow the light of the moon
And be guided by the North Star in the sky
They prayed for Harriet Tubman or William Still to come and guide them to freedom
As they had helped many others escape the captivity of this institution of slavery
They prayed for abolitionists such as Levi Coffin, John Fairfield, and the Quakers
To navigate them through secret routes and to safe houses during this journey to freedom
Like the Hebrews trying to reach the Promise Land
They knew the day was coming when they could tell their story of how they had gone from slavery to freedom
How they had gone from picking cotton and tobacco
And being branded as property and forced to be servants for life
To being truly free
They knew the day was coming when they could tell their story of how as a runaway slave they hid during the day and traveled at night
And avoided the alarms of the bloodhounds and their capture by bounty hunters
And how they rode that freedom train to freedom
Until they could say I am free at last! I'm truly free!

A Well-Kept Secret

A well-kept secret
A hidden story
A story that should not be unknown
But yet it is an unknown and untold story
The story of how our nation's capital was mostly built from the sweat and labor of Black men
Free and enslaved
Over 400 Black men helped to build the White House and our nation's capitol
Symbols of democracy
Symbols of liberty
Symbols of freedom
But yet these men did not know what true democracy, liberty and freedom were
America denied them of what America stood for
Even though they built the symbols for America, they were not recognized
A story that has been hidden for over 150 years
And America has not told and continues to not tell us this piece of American history
The story of America's most enduring symbols of freedom
Being mostly built from the free labor and cheap labor of Black men that America has failed to recognize or respect
Skilled and unskilled laborers
Bricklayers, carpenters, haulers, and stonecutters
Men that helped build America
And were committed to the assignment of making the nation's capital into what we see today
But little has been written about these Black men
The dedicated workers and forced laborers that built the nation's most symbolic structures remain America's great secret
As the bronze statue called "Freedom" sits atop the capitol dome
Little is told of Phillip Reid and the other Black men that placed the statue there

As we gaze up at the capitol and admire "Freedom"
We fail to realize "Freedom" owes a lot of her existence to these many Black men who did not know freedom
We must realize many Blacks for most of America's history never felt true freedom
Never felt true liberty
Never felt what it is like to be a true American
And had been denied the right to participate in true democracy
How can American history deny this story?
How can America not give due respect to these men?
You can read about the architects who designed these buildings
You can read about how these buildings are constructed
But you will not read about those Black men that actually built the nation's capital and these symbols of freedom for the world to see
Most of their names are unknown
They are not recognized and their contributions are unknown
And as American history is revealed
America must recognize there is some American history that still needs to be told
And there should not be any more well-kept secrets

One Great Day - The Pennsylvania Grand Review

When Johnny Comes Marching Home Again
Hurrah! Hurrah!
He was not recognized by his own country
Hurrah! Hurrah!
There was no celebration and there were no cheers
He fought for his country, but his country did not care
The shame of America
When Johnny Comes Marching Home

May 23rd and 24th of 1865 were not days of celebration for the African-American troops that fought for the Union during the Civil War like it was for the rest of the Union troops
After two long years of fighting to help save a divided nation
And answering the call to arms for their nation and for freedom
The almost 200,000 African-American troops were excluded from the Union's victory celebration over the Confederacy in the nation's capital
Excluded and uninvited by then President Andrew Johnson and the United States War Department from participating in the military recognition known as the Grand Review
Racism had denied these true patriots the recognition and tribute they deserved
Some of them free and some of them slaves, but as Americans and patriots they proved they were
True American patriots, but ignored, insulted, and unrecognized by their nation
The nation they fought for and were willing to die for when their nation needed them the most
The nation they valiantly represented had treated them like their efforts did not matter
And as though they did not play an important and vital role in the winning of the war that changed America forever

These African-American troops could wear their Union blue and serve their nation
They could cook, dig trenches, and bury their comrades in graves for their nation
They could carry the banner of their nation as they engaged in battle, despite the discrimination and injustice they faced because of the color of their skin
They were even massacred and murdered for the role they played for their nation by the Confederacy during war
But their nation failed to recognize them for their many contributions
And for their bravery, courage, loyalty, and sacrifices
Treating them with the same type of respect as the system they gave their lives to change
Sadly, their commitment to their nation and their quest for freedom did not change how they were treated
Because their treatment as American patriots in many ways was very similar to the psychological chains of slavery and of their second class citizenship in America
But some African-American women from Harrisburg, Pennsylvania who were members of the William Garnett Society
With the help of four leading African-Americans, Thomas Morris Chester, William Howard Day, Octavious Catto and Stephen Smith organized a day of recognition and remembrance
And November 14, 1865 was a great day for African Americans and for America
A day of recognition for the African American troops that fought and died for their country and for their freedom
Attracting African-American troops from twenty-five states
They were given their due recognition in the capital of the keystone state
As they paraded through the city of Harrisburg in their uniforms and were honored by the large gathering of people with cheers
They finally received the respect they deserved on that one great day

*But somehow this story has become a hidden piece of American history
And sadly an afterthought that is unknown not only to Americans,
But to most African-Americans
So let us not forget this powerful story of the Pennsylvania Grand Review
And how the African-American troops during the Civil War helped to make America what it is today*

Robert Smalls Was an American Hero

It is amazing how pieces of history sometimes become hidden in the many chapters of American history
People whose names should be household names
And historical facts that deserve to not be forgotten
Are often lost in between the then and the now
Hardly ever being acknowledged for a place in history
Nor given due recognition and respect for contributions whether good or bad to American history
As we trace the past to the present
A name that should stand out in American history is the name of Robert Smalls
Born a slave in Beaufort, South Carolina
The thought of dying a slave was not an option for Robert Smalls
And his desire for freedom for him and his family was very strong
So during the Civil War when the opportunity for freedom presented itself, he did not hesitate to chase it
In a daring escape, planned as if it was written for Hollywood Robert Smalls and seven other slave crewmen stole a Confederate war ship, the CSS Planter, in the early morning hours while the ship's crew slept on shore
He escaped from the slavery he had known all of his life
Being a trained seaman from his time working on the ship, he picked up his family and other slaves from a hidden dock
And maneuvered the ship through the Charleston Harbor past five Confederate forts that guarded the harbor
Northward, he navigated the ship armed with code books, and weapons
Dressed like the ship's captain and with knowledge of the correct whistle signals to identify the ship, he was allowed to pass through the harbor without any opposition
As he traveled the seven miles to freedom and towards the Union navy's blockade, he hoisted a white sheet as a flag and surrendered the ship to the Union navy

Robert Smalls and his family were free
Possessing a strong knowledge of the Charleston Harbor and the Confederate defenses, he was able to provide detailed information that would be valuable to the Union Navy
He was received as a national hero and was financially rewarded for the capture of a Confederate ship
He met with President Lincoln and helped convince him to accept African-Americans into the Union army
He later became the first African-American captain of an American ship, having been appointed captain of the very ship that sailed him to freedom
During the Civil War, Robert Smalls served in seventeen battle engagements
And though he was never officially enrolled in the military, his service as a civilian was exemplary
But this great story does not end there
After the war he returned to Beaufort, South Carolina and purchased his former master's house where he lived for the rest of his life
His charisma, way with words, and ability to articulate led him into politics and helped him to become the most powerful African-American in South Carolina
He became an elected official during Reconstruction and served five terms in Congress as the representative from South Carolina
He helped to found the Republican Party in South Carolina
He participated in the drafting of the post Civil War South Carolina state constitution during Reconstruction
He authored legislation that created in South Carolina the nation's first free public school system
He fought for equal travel accommodations for African-Americans
He spoke out against the disfranchisement of African-American voters
He dedicated his political life to fighting for racial equality and civil rights for African-Americans

He believed that all African-Americans needed was an equal chance in the battle of life
And if given that chance they would truly show America all they could be
His bravery and courage led him to freedom and helped African-Americans maintain a freedom in America
And though he had an unlikely passage to freedom, his life journey was his personal testimony that all people were supposed to be free
And somewhere in the shadows of the lost chapters of American history
You will find the name Robert Smalls, an American hero

I Am an African-American

I am an African-American
An adjective and a noun
A descendent of kings and queens
But I am also the offspring of the slave and the slave master
The product of a very rich history
But also the victim of a very painful and tragic history
I am an African-American
An adjective and a noun
In tune with who I am
Appreciating my darkness
Loving my darkness
And I am totally proud of my darkness
But I also understand the deepness of my darkness
And because of my darkness, I must be twice as good and work twice as hard
Just to reach my full potential
I am an African-American
An adjective and a noun
I have a history that helped to mold the world
With contributions affecting everything from human rights to science
From agriculture to countless inventions
But I am also scared by the African-American's past
I have a legacy of bondage and oppression
Many of my ancestors never knew freedom
And so many others died fighting for their freedom
Yet so many today do not appreciate the price that was paid for this freedom
I am an African-American
An adjective and a noun
I have a title that identifies who I am
A title that expresses my cultural and historical roots
A title that speaks of the journey of a stolen people
A title that expresses my pre- and post-slavery experience

*A title that says, "Yes! I am an American."
But also a title that strongly says I am from African descent
And even though Africa has never met me
My title reminds me that Africa will always be a part of me
I am an African-American
An adjective and a noun
A description that is beyond understanding
A description that has taught me what life really means
A description that breaks down the contradictions of America's democracy
A description that helps me to understand my past, present, and future
A description that helps me to deal with why I continue to be subjected to discrimination, prejudice, and racism
I am an African-American
An adjective and a noun
And I must never forget who I am*

Frederick Douglass

Frederick Douglass was born a slave
But he knew he was not born to be a slave
He knew no human being was created to be the property of another human being
And he was adamant about not being owned by anyone but God
His indictment on slavery and fight for freedom started as a young man
And this fight would last his whole life
His journey from slavery to freedom
As detailed in his autobiography,
"A Narrative of the Life of Frederick Douglass, an American Slave",
Started in bondage and ended with his freedom
After escaping from slavery
He became a voice for the freedom of his people
He published the newspaper "The North Star"
And became an abolitionist
Frederick Douglass became one of America's greatest advocates for human rights
He stated, "I would unite with anybody to do right and with nobody to do wrong"
He believed in America
He believed in the American constitution
He believed in the fight for emancipation
He believed in change
He realized that although he was free
He really was not free
Because his people were not free
A brilliant and outspoken speaker
He spoke of the freedom of descendants of Africa enslaved in America in his speech,
"What to the Slave is the Fourth of July?"
He stated, "This Fourth of July is yours, not mine. You may rejoice, I must mourn."

He asked, "Are the great principles of political freedom and of natural justice, embodied in that Declaration of Independence extended to us?"
He knew that freedom for his people would not come easily
He was strongly involved in the Underground Railroad
His home became an important station on the road to freedom for many slaves
He was an adviser and friend to President Abraham Lincoln
Challenging the President for the emancipation of the slaves
After the Civil War and the end of slavery
He continued to be an advocate for human rights
He fought for the adoption of constitutional amendments that guaranteed voting rights
He fought for the rights of women long before the women rights movement
He campaigned to end segregation in the Rochester, New York school system
He fought for America to be what it was founded to be
The land of the free
The moral vision of Frederick Douglass helped to not only change America
But it helped to shape America

They Were Called the Buffalo Soldiers

They were called the Buffalo Soldiers
By the Indians they were named and known
They helped America become America, but their place in American history is not very well recognized
They were commissioned to serve their country
But they were not respected in the land they called home
They carried the banner of America
Even though America did not always treat them like they were soldiers of its own
They fought and died for their country
This they did for their home
They truly served their nation
They represented their country as courageous, proud, and strong, soldiers
But when you look into American history, the story of the Buffalo Soldiers remains virtually unheard of
They were called the Buffalo Soldiers
By the Indians they were named and known
They helped America become America, but their place in American history is not very well recognized
They were mighty men of valor
Their contributions to America were strong
Their fighting style was fierce and they became known for their bravery
They were former slaves and they were free Black men, but most of all, they were American soldiers
They performed with honor and distinction
And they did this for the country they were commissioned to serve
But still America fails to tell their story or their role in how the West was won
They were called the Buffalo Soldiers
By the Indians they were named and known

They helped America become America, but their place in American history is not very well recognized
Despite their scant recognition and the lack of respect they received
They remained dedicated to America and their loyalty was true indeed
They escorted settlers westward and in most of the battles they fought in, they won
The Buffalo Soldiers served America
And American heroes they truly were
Sadly, they were admired more by the Apache, Cheyenne and Sioux Indians, whom they bravely fought, than by their own nation
A lost piece of American history about men whose stories have seldom been told
They were called the Buffalo Soldiers
By the Indians they were named and known
They helped America become America, but their place in American history is not very well recognized
Though they only had limited freedom and the discrimination and racism they felt was strong
They persevered and built a legacy that was proof that they belonged
And though you will not find much about them in the history books
The role they played in American history should be very strong
But sadly, in America's history they are just another unfamiliar story that is very seldom told
And they were called the Buffalo Soldiers
By the Indians they were named and known
They helped America become America, but unfortunately their place in American history is not very well recognized

The African-American Journey in America Tells a Story

With an identity deeply rooted in this land called America
The African-American journey in America tells a story
A story of courage, determination, perseverance and strength
A story that reaches from the past and touches the future
A story that travels up the steps from the depths of the slave ships and through almost 400 years of history in this land called America
A story that travels up Pennsylvania Avenue and to the entrance of the White House
A story that not only illuminates the realities of the African-American experience in America
But a story that tells of the dramatic journey and significant history of African-Americans
You cannot accurately describe the identity of America
Without showing the African-American contributions to America
You cannot accurately describe the identity of America
Without revealing the true depth of the African-American experience
You cannot accurately describe the identity of America
Without telling the story of the strength of African-Americans on their journey to freedom
Yes! The African-American journey in America tells a story
But unfortunately, the dissemination of this story has painted an inaccurate picture of America
And sadly, the mis-education of America has not allowed the whole story of America to be told
How can part of the past be denied and a great legacy be proclaimed?
But this is America and this is the legacy America wants to proclaim
Some of America's most significant history has been contributed by African-Americans

And African-American history has often been denied, excluded or lost during the developing of American history
We must tell the stories!
We must retrace the steps of the African-American journey!
We must do a roll call of the many contributors in the chapters of this distorted and incomplete story!
Because it seems almost like historic act after historic act had never occurred
So many stories lost and untold
How can we have so much history being heard by many for the very first time!
What would America's legacy be in this sweet land of liberty without the acts and history of African-Americans!
Those that cultivated the land and helped to build a nation
How can we absorb the greatness of America without absorbing all of America's past!
Without absorbing the journey of African-Americans
Without explaining and bringing understanding to the meaning of the African-American experience in America from America's beginning
As history speaks, let us allow accuracy and truth to be the foundation for America and its legacy
Let us open the book and rediscover the true American history that has been forgotten
And as we examine and study this open book, let us embrace the good and the bad of America's past, because both helped to define America
And as the past, present, and future connect
Let this path pave the way to fully understanding America and its legacy
And let this be the end of the distorted view of America
And the beginning of the full acceptance of an America that understands its past and truly embraces its legacy

Up from Slavery - Booker T. Washington

Booker T. Washington came up from slavery
And he became one of the most influential men of his time
Born a slave
But knowing he was not meant to be a slave
His hunger for freedom and knowledge provided him with the motivation
The motivation to become an American educator, author, and advisor to presidents
All while coming up from slavery
Booker T. Washington was a leader and spokesman for the African-American community
He was a leader during a time when there were few voices advocating for the rights of African- Americans
He believed in the transformation of his people
He believed in his people being fully accepted as citizens of America
He believed in the awakening of his people
And he believed that acceptance into mainstream America for African-Americans could best be obtained through education and a philosophy of self-help
Booker T. Washington believed in his people
And even though his people were just coming out of slavery
He saw the potential of his people
He could see his people playing a role in the future of America
Being a visionary, he believed in the future of his people
And he knew education was the key to achieving a better future
And no one pushed education harder for African-Americans than Booker T. Washington
He created an educational model that helped African-Americans rise up from the intellectual, mental, physical, and economic effects of slavery

He founded Tuskegee Institute as an educational center for academic learning
His focus on agricultural and industrial training taught many former slaves professional skills and trades
He helped to start and operate over 5000 community schools throughout the South
He worked hard to improve the conditions of African-Americans
Booker T. Washington showed America through a commitment to education and industry there was a place for African-Americans in America
Dedicating himself to helping African-Americans on their journey towards freedom and equality
During Post-Reconstruction when Blacks were the victims of discrimination, racism and hate crimes
He had an impact on race relations
He used his political influence to fight for the constitutional rights of African-Americans and gave financial support in the legal fights against inequality and the Jim Crow laws
He spoke out against lynching and injustice
And he worked hard to make a separate America more equal
Booker T. Washington was one of the most influential men of his time
Despite his journey up from slavery
He helped to change America
And his life was an example that became his legacy

Reconstruction

How could there be reconstruction?
If the foundation of America was not developed so that all people in America could be citizens of America and be treated equally in America
How could there be reconstruction?
The birth of a nation gave birth to the institution of slavery and failed to give basic human rights to an enslaved people
America! America!
With a look at your history
A Pre-Reconstruction history that painted a clear picture of the brokenness of America
In retrospect, Pre-Reconstruction divided a nation and started a war
So how could there be Reconstruction when you have Pre-Reconstruction
They call the period after the Civil War, Reconstruction
Yes! The war ended slavery
And the unfinished business of the Emancipation Proclamation was completed
And Reconstruction created an avenue for the return of those states that left the union
But Reconstruction struggled to receive four million former slaves as citizens of this great nation
For a short period of time, Reconstruction gave former slaves civil rights and allowed them to vote, participate in the political process and to feel like a human being
Reconstruction brought new laws, constitutional amendments, and statutes
The 13th Amendment abolished slavery
The 14th Amendment guaranteed citizenship to all persons born or naturalized in America
The 15th Amendment gave the right to vote to American citizens
And in 1867, former slaves voted for the first time
During Reconstruction over 1500 former slaves held public office

But free at last did not mean free at last
And Reconstruction had its resistance
During the 1870's, Southern Democrats calling themselves Redeemers, regained control and power of the Southern state governments
And through acts of intimidation from white supremacist groups such as the Ku Klux Klan, Red Shirts and the White League
And violent attacks such as public lynching and race riots like the Colfax Massacre brought the return of Dixie and led to the disfranchisement of Southern Blacks
Reconstruction's weaknesses lead to the birth of Post-Reconstruction
The compromise of 1877 gave Rutherford B. Hayes and the Republicans the White House, but it gave the Southern Democrats the old South back
And the end of Reconstruction marked the beginning of Jim Crow
Jim Crow became the law of the land in the South
Southern states soon passed new constitutions, laws and enacted the restrictive "black codes" that treated Blacks as second class citizens
Losing many of their rights and the ability to vote, Blacks soon lost all gains achieved during Reconstruction
The system of sharecropping and its permanent indebtedness guaranteed servitude
The sad reality was Post-Reconstruction was almost as bad as Pre-Reconstruction and slavery
No rights, no suffrage, and a return to being an oppressed people
And during the next eighty years this was the way of life for Blacks in the South
When it was supposed to be Reconstruction

The Wilmington Race Riot- A Day of Blood and Terror

Most of America has never heard of this episode in American history
Because it has been a chapter in American history that has been hidden quite well
This piece of American history is so shocking; the validity of the story would be questioned
But what happened on November 10, 1898 in Wilmington, NC is a true story
And the events of that day really happened
On this day, democracy and freedom were taken
And on this day, we have the only occurrence of an elected government being overthrown in the history of the United States
It has been called a race riot, but it was more like a coup d'état
A rebellion and revolt against a government chosen by the people and for the people
A massacre and the running out of town of those people who were elected to lead the city
A day of blood
A day of terror
And though they were well informed of the events that occurred on this day
The President of the United States did nothing to stop it
And the Governor of the State of North Carolina did nothing to stop it
On this day, democracy in America was betrayed
In 1898, Wilmington, NC was the largest city in the state and was a thriving port city
During America's Reconstruction, era, the majority of the city's population was African-American
The African-American community during this time was full of successful business owners and they played a vital role in the city's politics as well as in the city's economic success

By working cohesively with many progressive whites who were members of the Populist and Republican Parties
African-American's involvement in the city's political process helped to take away the long held political grip the Democratic Party had on the city
And with its active base of African-American voters, Wilmington, NC was an example of what true democracy should look like in America
Throughout America, Wilmington, NC was a symbol of pride for African-Americans
But everyone in America was not warm to this new form of American emocracy
And to the new freedom and rights African-Americans had gained during the Reconstruction era
The racial parity in Wilmington inflamed racial resentment and tension
And set in motion the wheels that lead to the events on this day that became a historical secret
The Old South had lost control of the government in the election of 1896
But now the Old South was ready to take the government and Wilmington, NC back
A day of blood
A day of terror
A campaign focused on white fears and paranoia instigated by the media and encouraged by those that wanted a return of the Old South sparked the flames of hate on this day
With an agitated mob gathering of over 2000 people
The city of Wilmington, NC was attacked and its government overthrown
The city's mayor, council members and other city officers, were forced to resign and leave town
The editor of the city's African-American newspaper whose editorial on race relations became a tool that helped to heighten white anger was chased out of town and his office burned down

African-Americans were hunted down and killed like wild game on a hunting trip
And many city buildings and businesses were burned to the ground and destroyed
The agitated crowd of rioters posed proudly in front of the frames of burned out buildings
The exact number of lives lost on this day is unknown, but many lives were lost and it was reported the Cape Fear River was full of bodies giving it the name the "Bloody Cape"
In the days following this uprising and tragic event, hundreds of people - both Black and White - were forced to leave the city
A new city government was established and recognized by the State of North Carolina
And for the next seventy years a political system was implemented that strangled the rights and dreams of African-Americans and created a system of powerlessness
Introducing the birth of the Jim Crow social order and the white supremacy era that intimidated and terrorized African-Americans for generations
It marked a turning point in American history that introduced the beginning of American racial terrorism
Setting the stage throughout America for similar race riots in Atlanta, Tulsa, Rosewood and Springfield
Making Jim Crow laws a way of life throughout the South
Taking away the African-American's right to vote
Disfranchising African-Americans
And introducing African-Americans to state-sanctioned racial terror throughout the country
A day of blood
A day of terror
And a day that became the shame of American democracy
Changed America
And it took America almost a century to even remember and acknowledge the events that occurred on that day
But November 10, 1898 is still one of America's hidden secrets
And it was a day of blood

And it was a day of terror

Lynching Is Also American History

How do you remember painful portions of American history?
How do you bring to light the painful portions of the past without feeling the pain?
How do you deal with the subject of lynching without dealing with the reality of the act?
When over three thousand African-Americans have lost their lives over the past one hundred years to this violent and hateful act
And to this form of illegal execution
Lynching, unfortunately, is a part of America's history
America's hidden and ugly legacy
For a period, lynching was as American as apple pie
There were no laws prohibiting this shameful tradition
Nor were there any crusades for justice
Because when it came to Judge Charles Lynch's justice
There was no jury of the peers
There was no with "Liberty and Justice for All," as our pledge of allegiance to America states
Because lynching in America was America's method of terrorism
A pre-meditated act by angry mobs and hate groups such as the Ku Klux Klan
Who used lynching as a way to intimidate and scare fearful African-Americans
Unfortunately and tragically, so many people were victims of this type of mob justice
Often being accused of crimes exaggerated or of crimes that did not occur at all
And sometimes even becoming a victim because they were simply in the wrong place at the wrong time
No convictions?
No justice?
No laws?
No protection?
Just a sentencing of death by hanging

Victims often having their eyes gouged out, teeth pulled, beaten, burned, dismembered or castrated
And sadly, this reign of terror was a part of America's history
Let the truth be told – lynchings were big events in some parts of the country
People often gathered to watch the lynchings with its entertainment-like atmosphere
With the lynchings often being photographed for pictures that were made into postcards
And victim's body parts were often sold as souvenirs
Just imagine the crowd as they entertained the hanging of a lifeless body
Throughout the nation, but especially in the South, these acts reached epidemic proportions
And even African-American soldiers who served their country in war were being lynched in their uniforms
And that was not even enough to make America end these hate crimes or the illegal death sentences that were so often done
Thousands of victims accused, convicted, and executed without a trial
And this was acceptable throughout America
Because after slavery and up until the end of the Civil Rights Movement, "hang them high" was common in many places in America
And sadly, lynching is also American history

America

America
The self proclaimed model to the world of democracy, freedom and liberty
A nation that was built by the people and for the people
A nation where there is a statue that is a symbol of liberty
A nation where the Declaration of Independence is a symbol of freedom
A nation where the Constitution and Bill of Rights are symbols of justice
Symbols of democracy, liberty, freedom and justice
But America has been hypocritical
Because America has not always been an example of democracy, liberty, freedom and justice for all
America has not always stood for the doctrine and philosophy that America was built on
When we examine the history of America we will see that America has not always given democracy, liberty, freedom and justice to all
Especially the African-American people
For African-Americans, we must ask the questions!
What democracy?
What liberty?
What freedom?
What justice?
From America's beginning to now
Even America must admit African-Americans have been done wrong
African-Americans have been the victims of slavery and being treated less than human
African-Americans have been the victims of racism, discrimination, and prejudice
African-Americans have been the victims of lynchings, hate crimes, murders, and the acts of American racial terrorism

And African-Americans, after almost 400 years, continue to be victims
Victims of the disparities of America's version of democracy, liberty, freedom and justice
How can America preach democracy, liberty, freedom, and justice?
But today have a Jena Six
How can America still have a Genarlow Wilson and the Scott Sisters?
For African-Americans, we must ask
What democracy?
What liberty?
What freedom?
What justice?
How can America say it stands for democracy, liberty, freedom, and justice?
When there is still a problem with getting justice in America
How can America say it stands for democracy, liberty, freedom and justice?
When there are inequalities in education and with employment
How can America claim it stands for democracy, liberty, freedom and justice?
And not practice freedom and liberty
How can America say it stands for democracy, liberty, freedom, and justice?
When Trayvon Martin is dead
And for African-Americans, we must ask
What democracy?
What liberty?
What freedom?
What justice?

What Is in a Name?

What is in a name?
To a race of people that had its original names taken away
Enslaved, tortured, and beaten until they no longer acknowledged who they were
Forced to accept the names of their oppressors and to forget their true identity
Creating an identity crisis that lasted almost 400 years
What is in a name?
To a race of people whose journey was worse than the Holocaust, Apartheid or any act of genocide this world has ever seen
To a group of people that was stolen from its homeland
And experienced a nightmare that was beyond understanding
But today have many of the slave owners' last names that tells the story of what America has forgotten
What is in a name?
When your name is supposed to identify who you are and is a symbol of heritage and pride
But in reality, the name tells the stories of the ancestors of many people's challenging past since coming to America
And how names like Washington, Jefferson, Jackson, and Taylor are constant reminders of the sins of America's slave owning founding fathers!
The names that are reminders of the African-American experience in America
What is in a name?
When a name describes how a race of people have evolved in how they are identified in America
From Colored to Negro to Black to African-American
And let us not forget that term nigger
A term that has gone from the most hateful name you could call an African-American
To a term of endearment which I do not understand
But I can only believe it is part of the mental and psychological damage done to a group of people whose experience and journey

has caused them to hate themselves so much they would used that term
Because how can you call yourself or someone else a nigger and be proud of it
What is in a name?
A great deal when it tells of the plight and struggles of a people
And how it is the historical connection of a race that helped to build America
A race that has suffered and died for America
A race whose name should define their place in America
What is in a name?
When it reminds you of the Middle Passage and the scars and long term effects of slavery
When it reminds you of Jim Crow laws, segregation and the posted "White Only" signs
When it reminds you of a journey older than America
What is in a name?
When it reminds you of the road that was traveled to freedom
And how freedom was not the same for all people
And how everyone did not come to America through Ellis Island
It reminds you of the great racial divide and the disparity that continues to exist in America
It reminds you of how far a race has come because of its journey
And even though Black people in America have been stripped of the ability and historical connections to fully identify who they truly are
A name says so much
For a people that had so much taken away from them their names now give them TRUTH
The real truth for them individually and as a race
The names tell the stories of the past, present and future
The names tell the good and the bad of their journey as a people
The names tell who they are
That is what is in a name for African-Americans

W.E.B. Du Bois Was a Voice

W.E.B. Du Bois was a voice
A voice during a time when African-Americans were expected to be silent
A voice during a time when there were few African-Americans voicing their thoughts and opinions on the conditions and state of Black America
A voice during a time when speaking out could often bring life threatening consequences and other problems for African Americans
A voice during a time when African-Americans were treated as second class citizens in the country they called home
W.E.B. Du Bois was a voice
A voice for African-American's future to look much different than their past and present
A voice for African-Americans to be respected and allowed to reach their full potential in America
W.E.B. Du Bois was a voice
A voice of courage
A voice of racial pride
A voice for change
As an activist, author, educator, historian, sociologist, and fighter for racial equality
W.E.B. Du Bois fought to make a difference
W.E.B. Du Bois fought to change America
As a graduate of Fisk University
As the first African-American to earn a Doctorate from Harvard University
As a leader in higher education and the social sciences
As a leader in the Niagara Movement
As a leader in the National Association for the Advancement of Colored People
As a leader in the Pan-African Movement
W.E.B. Du Bois was a voice
As editor of the publication "The Crisis"

As the author of over twenty books
As the author of over more than four thousand articles and essays published
As worded in his poem of faith and vision for change in the "Credo"
W.E.B. Du Bois was a voice
Through his belief that higher education and the developing of a "Talented Tenth" within the African-American race would help to close the racial divide in America
Through his advocacy for civil, human, and racial justice
Through his studies of history, economics, politics, and race
Through his research in the socio-economic development of African-Americans
W.E.B. Du Bois was a voice
A voice that became one of the most prominent fighters for the rights of African-Americans in the twentieth century
A voice that brought the cultural, political, and social relevance of African-Americans to the attention of the world
A voice that challenged and questioned America on the issues of African-Americans on all grounds and on America's resistance to change
A voice that encouraged African-American creativity in the arts and in the writing of stories and poetry
W.E.B. Du Bois was a voice

To Be Black Is Reason to Be Proud

Black is beautiful
And to be Black is reason to be proud!
History so strong
Contributions so many
Blacks have affected everything in America
From medicine to government
Education to entertainment
Blacks are the embryo to civilization
The alpha to so much
History and contributions can be traced back to the birth of America
And Blacks are still playing a strong role in making America the nation it is today
Black is beautiful
And to be Black is reason to be proud!
As beautiful as the slaves' dreams for freedom
As beautiful as the published works of a slave girl named Phyllis Wheatley
As beautiful as the shining of the North Star that guided so many slaves to freedom
As beautiful as Frederick Douglass' efforts in the abolition of slavery
As beautiful as the tears of joy flowing down the face of someone tasting freedom for the first time
Black is beautiful
And to be Black is reason to be proud!
As beautiful as Booker T. Washington's "Up from Slavery"& W.E.B. Du Bois' "Souls of Black Folks" and their courage to speak strongly for the rights of their people
As beautiful as what came to be known as Lincoln University - the first institution of higher learning for Blacks
As beautiful as Nicodemus, Kansas being the first all-black community established in America

As beautiful as Dr. Daniel Hale Williams successfully performing the first open heart surgery
As beautiful as George Washington Carver changing the world with his advances in agriculture and research
As beautiful as Paul Laurence Dunbar's literary description of rural Black life in America
Black is beautiful
And to be Black is reason to be proud!
As beautiful as James Weldon Johnson's words in "Lift Every Voice and Sing"
As beautiful as the social thoughts, culture, and creativity of the Harlem Renaissance
As beautiful as the words of Langston Hughes, Claude McKay, and Zora Neale Hurston
As beautiful as the music that came from the soul of Billie Holiday, Marian Anderson and Mahalia Jackson
As beautiful as Carter G. Woodson establishing the recognition of the contributions of Blacks in America
Black is beautiful
And to be Black is reason to be proud!
As beautiful as the Tuskegee Airmen beating the odds of becoming pilots and defending their country proudly
As beautiful as Marian Anderson performing at the New York Metropolitan Opera
As beautiful as the end of "Separate but Equal"
As beautiful as the grace shown by Jackie Robinson as he integrated professional baseball
As beautiful as John Hope Franklin's "From Slavery to Freedom" told Black people's story in American history
As beautiful as the poetry of Maya Angelou, Nikki Giovanni, Sonia Sanchez, and Alice Walker
Black is beautiful
And to be Black is reason to be proud!
As beautiful as thousands gathered at the Lincoln Memorial to hear "I Have a Dream"

As beautiful as thousands of Black men gathered at the Lincoln Memorial to unite and to reveal a vastly different picture of the Black man in America
As beautiful as the record setting crowd of people gathered to watch the taking of oath of the first Black President of the United States of America
As beautiful as God's many complexions and shades that define and make up how being Black is beautiful
Because Black is beautiful
And to be Black is reason to be proud!

The Flag

When I look at the confederate flag
I see hate
I see racism
I see discrimination
I see the ugliness of the flag
When I look at the confederate flag
I see treason
I see anti-America
I see the splitting of a nation
I see slavery
When I look at the confederate flag
I see violence
I see murder
I see lynching
I see terrorism
When I look at the confederate flag
I see the Ku Klux Klan
I see crosses burning
I see the night stalkers
I see the fear of victims
When I look at the confederate flag
I see the ignorance
I see the law breakers
I see the crimes
When I look at the confederate flag
I must ask how people that calls themselves Americans
Can view this flag as a symbol of American pride
And as a symbol of American patriotism
When I look at the confederate flag
I must ask how anyone can honor a symbol of hate
That has a history of rebellion, intimidation, and torture
When I look at the confederate flag

*I really do not know how anyone can be so emotionally attached
to a symbol that goes against so much of what America
represents
A symbol that divides America instead of uniting America
When I look at the confederate flag
I must remind myself
The battle is not over and the journey is not complete
Because even though it has stars and stripes
And is red, white, and blue
The confederate flag is entrenched in hatred and racism
And a look at its history will reveal that this is true
The confederate flag!*

America Must Pay

America must pay
For the crime that it has committed against African-Americans
America must pay
For the crimes of kidnapping, slavery, murder, assault, threats of terror, oppression, and discrimination
America must pay
For the psychological and mental abuse of over 400 years of slavery and oppression committed by America
America must pay and reparations are due
African-Americans have been the victims of the Trans-Atlantic slave trade
One of the greatest atrocities in the history of the world
With millions of Africans losing their lives
And all the victims that survived the slave trade were taken from their homelands and lost their families and culture
America must pay
These victims of this long voyage across the Atlantic Ocean were brought to a foreign land and were enslaved
They served as free labor
With much of America being built for free by these victims of forced labor
They helped to develop America agriculturally, commercially, and industrially
But has America compensated the ancestors of these people? No!
America must pay
After slavery, African-Americans were still treated cruelly and with hostility
They were forced to live in fear in a country that failed to accept them and treat them with respect
And even though slavery and the title of slave were no longer legal
They were still treated as badly as when they were slaves and America refused to look at African-Americans as Americans

They were denied their basic human rights and their civil rights
They were not given any of the necessary resources needed to be an independent people
They had no land, no money, and no power
America must pay
African-Americans have been subjected to over 400 years of discrimination, lynching, racism and segregation
And African-Americans have paid a price
They have lost their culture, history, and much of their true identity
America must pay
The African-Americans have been the victims of cultural, mental, physical, and spiritual destruction
And America has yet to pay its debt
Are African-Americans given the respect of the Japanese, Jewish, and Polish people?
No! Because all of those groups were given reparations for the atrocities and genocide against their people
And none of those acts were as atrocious or lasted as long as the acts against African-Americans
America owes something more than an apology
America must pay reparations to the victims of the greatest holocaust ever
America must pay

How Did African-American History Become Irrelevant?

How does history become irrelevant?
When it is African-American history!
The dream and efforts of Carter G. Woodson
The father of recognizing the neglected past of African-Americans
Has become a forgotten time of remembrance
From Negro History week
To Black History month
To February now becoming a month that we hardly take the time to recognize and remember the past achievements and accomplishments of African-Americans
February has even become a month to disrespect the legacy of African-Americans
From a month of remembrance
To a month of Black exploitation and negative themed films being presented as significant African-American history
From a month of celebration
To a month of ignoring the journey of African-Americans
From a month of remembering the price that was paid for freedom
To a month of selective amnesia and an inability to remember that freedom was not free
From a twenty-eight day shout out on the history of African-Americans
To twenty-eight days of a distorted view of American history
History has become distorted
How can a major part of American history become an afterthought?
How do we forget about African-Americans' contributions to America?
How do we forget about African-Americans' role in the making of America?

How can American history be complete without African-American history being accurate?
From 1619 until now
From chains to freedom
And we have gone from attempting to recognize all of that history in twenty-eight days
And let us not forget that extra day in leap years
To barely acknowledging or recognizing African-American history at all
So much history untold
When did African-American history become replaced by the promotion of negativity?
Every February we see less recognition and remembering of the African-American's past
Every February we hear less about the journey of African-Americans
And every February we see corporations marketing their interpretation of the recognition of African-American history
When did movies promoting crime, violence, and sex become an important piece of African-American history?
How did African-American history degenerate into an annual debate over if honoring the history of African-Americans is even necessary anymore?
How could African-Americans allow their history to be ignored or forgotten?
The recognition of African-American history was important to Carter G. Woodson
Because he understood having a knowledge and understanding of the past shaped and defined the present and the future
Carter G. Woodson understood why African-American history had to be relevant
He understood the journey to freedom was not easy and many had fought and died for that freedom
He understood knowing the past could help change the future
Carter G. Woodson understood the past and saw the future

And he understood the importance of not allowing the history of African-Americans to become irrelevant

The Harlem Renaissance

How can you define a period of time that truly cannot be defined?
How can you describe a period that is so broad in scope that it is indescribable!
How do you name a movement that impacted the world?
You define it, describe it and name it the Harlem Renaissance
A period of African-American artistic, cultural, and intellectual creativity
A period of racial expression and racial pride
A period that introduced the world to the African-American experience and perspective
This was the Harlem Renaissance
During a time when America's racial climate treated African-Americans like second class citizens
And racial segregation and Jim Crow laws painted a not so beautiful picture of two Americas based on race
The Harlem Renaissance created a racial identity and an avenue for the expression of cultural, social, and political freedom for African-Americans
During the 1920's and 1930's, the Harlem Renaissance movement had a profound impact on American history
Without the Harlem Renaissance movement
Would we have had the literary, magical words of James Weldon Johnson, Jessie Fauset and Zora Neale Hurston?
Without the Harlem Renaissance movement
Would we have had the inspiration of the poetry of Langston Hughes, Claude McKay, Jean Toomer, and Countee Cullen?
Without the Harlem Renaissance movement
Would we have had the addressing of political and social issues through the conscious and thought provoking writings of E. Franklin Frazier and Alain Locke?
Without the Harlem Renaissance
Would we have had some of the biggest influences not only to African-American culture, but to American culture?

The Harlem Renaissance symbolized a change in America
A change that affected the full spectrum of the American experience
From the literary arts to the visual arts
From drama, dance, and music to the politics and social issues of America
The Harlem Renaissance was the past, present, and future of African-Americans
The Harlem Renaissance was a symbol of courage and consciousness for African-Americans
The Harlem Renaissance symbolized when African-Americans had the freedom to express their thoughts and to tell their stories
The Harlem Renaissance was when African-Americans had the ability to creatively express themselves in the arts
The Harlem Renaissance was about the journey of a people who up until then lacked an avenue or voice to express who they were
The Harlem Renaissance was more than a fashion statement, creative art, powerful words and all that jazz
The Harlem Renaissance was a piece of American history that helped to develop and define America into the America we know today

Marcus Garvey - The Father of Black Nationalism

A journey into Black history will reveal the story of the father of Black Nationalism
A journey through the history of Black people will introduce a man who changed the mentality of Black people in America
A journey through Black history will introduce Marcus Mosiah Garvey
He was a leader during a period in America's past when there were few Black leaders with mass appeal
He was a charismatic leader
Marcus Garvey devoted his life to uniting Black people
He believed Black people should be free to determine their own destiny
So he gave them hope and a message to believe
"One God, One Aim and One Destiny"
Though his people were free
America's treatment of Blacks did not resemble true freedom
And though they were deeply rooted in this land called America
Marcus Garvey envisioned redefining the identity of those of African descent
Being a great orator and a bold and passionate advocate of racial pride
He helped Black people to believe that being Black was beautiful
Marcus Garvey believed that Black people needed to be lifted up
Being a fierce and outspoken advocate for social, political, and economic freedom
He challenged Black people to dream
He challenged Black people to become self-sufficient
He challenged Black people to rise up and accomplish what they will
Through his Universal Negro Improvement Association and African Communities League

Marcus Garvey used a Pan-African philosophy to unite Black people
Connecting people of African descent throughout the world to Africa and its people
From Africa to America and back again
He was the first to lead a mass movement of Black people
Giving millions of Black people a sense of dignity and pride
He believed uniting Black people was the only way to improve the state and conditions of Black people
Marcus Garvey was driven to change the living experiences of Black people worldwide
Through the total redemption and liberation of his people
He believed his people needed a great awakening
He believed in Black Nationalism
And he devoted his life to this vision
And though he was never able to see his dream become reality
The dream of Marcus Garvey to unify Black people around the world inspired and motivated many to keep the memory of his efforts alive
He showed Black America how strong the race could be when they were united
And he taught Black people how to have a pride and a love for themselves that they had never known
So when we journey through Black history we will be introduced to Marcus Mosiah Garvey - the father of Black Nationalism

Black Ball - A League of Their Own

America's national past time did not always look the way it does today
During a time when "white only" laws were a part of everyday life in America
And America was a nation split by color
With a great racial divide between Blacks and Whites
Affecting everything from education to transportation to where you could eat
Blacks were treated as second class citizens in their own country
But sadly this was America
And unfortunately America's national past time was not excluded
Segregated
Discriminated
Prohibited
And forced to play the game they loved in leagues of their own
The Negro Leagues were born
Because due to the color of their skin
Blacks were barred from the major leagues
The sting of racial segregation would not allow them in
Playing in games where only the ball was white
From Atlanta to Memphis to New York
From Harrisburg to Cincinnati to Chicago
Black ball became the national past time for Blacks in America
They had their own teams
They had their own players
They had their own fans
They had their own leagues
They were the Negro Leagues
In the face of segregation, they packed stadiums and ball parks wherever they played
And people came from everywhere to see them play
Teams like the Pittsburgh Crawfords, Homestead Grays, Harrisburg Giants, and Kansas City Monarchs

Had a profound impact on the Black Community
Inspiring a feeling of pride in the face of diversity
Teams such as the Philadelphia Stars, Baltimore Elite Giants, and Birmingham Black Barons
Became the entertainment that united Black communities across America
With future Hall-of-Famers including Satchel Paige, Josh Gibson and Cool Papa Bell
Their performance on the field became legendary
They were some of the best baseball players to ever play the game, but unfortunately many of their names remained unfamiliar
They were robbed of the recognition and opportunities they truly deserved and dreamed about
They failed to receive the credit for their contribution to America's national past time
Ray Dandridge, Oscar Charleston, Buck Leonard, Biz Mackey and Ted "Double Duty" Radcliffe made the game special
Rube Foster, Mule Suttles, and Turkey Stearnes, together with many others, help to create the reputation that Black baseball players could play the game well
They played the game they loved with passion
Putting their abilities, hearts, and souls on the field
And though they received very little recognition and respect for their efforts
And many were never able to have their dreams of playing the game they loved at the highest level fulfilled
They paved the way for Jackie Robinson and many others
Their legacy helped to change the game and America forever
And it is all because they had to play black ball in a league of their own

Her Name Was Mary McLeod Bethune

Her name was Mary McLeod Bethune
And when you take a moment to absorb the history of America
The discovery of how important this woman's role in helping to change America will be revealed
During a time when America was a little different and the racial divide ran deep
Mary McLeod Bethune opened doors of opportunity
She carried the guiding light on the path that helped to pave the way towards a new day
She believed, preached and taught that change in America could be gained through equality in education
She fought tirelessly for a change in America that would affect all generations to come
An ambassador of inter-racial goodwill she knew no racial barriers
As an educator, civil rights leader and advisor to presidents she believed in a new day and a brighter future
Mary McLeod Bethune believed in America
One of fifteen children and the daughter of former slaves
She was working in the cotton and rice fields by the age of five
After she was introduced to education as a child, she developed a passion for learning
And this was the beginning of her love affair with education
She was able to attend college with the help of benefactors with a dream of one day becoming a missionary in Africa
But missionary work in Africa wasn't the calling for Mary McLeod Bethune
Because she had a higher calling that gave her a voice and a platform to lift up a people and a nation
After completing her education she founded a school for African-American girls
Her school grew from six girls to become what is known today as Bethune-Cookman University in Daytona Beach, Florida

An institution for higher learning with standards of education that could rival any school
She did this during a time when women were seldom seen in the leadership role as a college president
Through her guidance and leadership as school president she gained national prominence
Her students became her family and they often referred to her as "Mama Bethune"
She knew there was power with being educated
And as an educator she stressed the importance and value of being an educated African- American
She dedicated her life to the education of not only African-American people, but of all people
But Mary McLeod Bethune was more than just an educator
She was an advocate for change in America
She was an advocate for equality
She was a fighter for true freedom and justice in America
Mary McLeod Bethune was a fearless voice for what was right
And spoke out strongly against segregation and the wrongs of America
She battled courageously for voting rights, better jobs and equal rights for African-Americans
As President of the National Council of Negro Women she fought for the rights of African-American women
As an advisor to President Roosevelt she was a part of what came to be known as the Black Cabinet
An advisory board that addressed many issues affecting African-American people in America
She was the first African-American woman to head a federal agency
And her roles with the National Youth Administration and the Division of Negro Affairs helped to train and employ many African-Americans
She was committed to lifting up people to be all they could be Because she believed in people

Her dedication, guidance, influence and leadership pushed America a step closer towards true democracy
Mary McLeod Bethune became a shining star during a dark period in America's history
During a time when African-Americans, much less a person with darker skin as herself, was subjected to second class citizenship in America
She stood proud, strong and tall
She held her head high during a time when African-Americans were taught to hold their heads down
She dedicated her life and invested in the lives of many people to make America a great nation
A united nation for all people
Her contributions to America were many
And all of America has been blessed by the contribution of this great woman in American history
And her name was Mary McLeod Bethune

Charles Hamilton Houston Believed in America

Charles Hamilton Houston knew one thing
As long as "separate but equal" existed
Blacks in America would be treated similar to second class Americans
He knew if America was going to be America for everyone
Then America must change and this change must be supported by the law of the land
Charles Hamilton Houston dedicated his life to changing America
And his battlefield to attack and defeat the "separate but equal" doctrine would be the courtrooms of America's highest court
Charles Hamilton Houston knew if he could change the law
Then America could be changed
Being a visionary, he knew the time had come to deal with America's race issues
Houston understood the constitution and laws of America
Houston understood the Jim Crow laws and politics that became the backbone of the Supreme Court's Plessy versus Ferguson decision of 1896
And he saw the law as the weapon to challenge racial segregation and inequality
Before the Brown versus Board of Education decision of 1954
Before Thurgood Marshall and nine high school students in Little Rock, Arkansas
And before the Civil Rights Act of 1964
There was the architect to the legal challenge to end segregation in America
There was Charles Hamilton Houston
As Dean of the Howard University Law School, he trained and developed future lawyers in what we now know as Civil Rights law

He understood the training of Black lawyers was essential in dismantling the segregation laws that existed in America
As Chief Attorney to the NAACP, he planned the legal war to end racial inequality in America
He assembled a team comprised of the finest Black lawyers in America to attack legal segregation
He believed the weakest link in the chain of segregation was education
And that focusing on education was the key to defeating the "separate but equal" doctrine in America
He declared there was no such thing as "separate but equal", because segregation in itself imported inequality.
He believed a precedent could be established with enough small victories in the courts of America
And that all forms of segregation could eventually be declared unconstitutional
Between 1930 and the 1954 Brown decision, Charles Hamilton Houston played a role in nearly every Civil Rights case that went before the US Supreme Court
And even though he paved the road and laid the groundwork to end legal segregation in America
This fighter for equality, freedom, and justice died before seeing his dream become reality
And though he never saw his efforts and work to fruition
He knew the importance of his cause and how it would change the future of America
Charles Hamilton Houston the lawyer, teacher, pioneer, and man knew his journey and fight for equality and justice would not be in vain
Charles Hamilton Houston believed in America and what it could one day be

Lloyd Gaines Was an American Mystery

Unfortunately, America is a nation with many of unsolved mysteries
As you travel down the road of America's past
You will uncover a story that is hidden within the history of America
You will come across the story of a true American mystery
You will stumble upon the story of a man and of a case that helped to change America
It is the story of a man and of a case that is not well remembered or well known
It is the story of not only an unsolved mystery, but an obscure story that is a part of America's past
If you travel down the road of America's past
You will discover a story of the fight for equality
A story of bravery and perseverance
A story of race and justice
A story that helped to open the gates for change
And set a precedent for cases to come that would help to dismantle legal segregation in America
But you will also discover a story that is a reminder of America's resistance to change
If you travel down the road of America's past, you will discover the story of Lloyd Lionel Gaines
A man who only wanted to fulfill his dream of becoming a lawyer
A man who only wanted to be all he could be in America - the land of the free
During a time when slavery could still be seen in the rear view mirror
Jim Crow was very much alive and well in the South
The doctrine of "separate but equal" was the law of the land
And freedom was not all it was promised to be for Blacks in America

The journey down the road of America's past cannot totally conceal the story of Lloyd Gaines
Of how after graduating with honors from Lincoln University in Missouri, he was denied an opportunity to pursue his dream of attending Law School at the University of Missouri
He was denied because of the color of his skin
And because America was not quite ready for change
But Lloyd Gaines fought for his right to an equal education
And with the assistance and leadership of the NAACP and its lawyer, Charles Hamilton Houston
The Gaines versus Canada case of 1938 was seen as a way to challenge the "Plessy versus Ferguson" decision of 1896 that created the foundation for "separate but equal"
The case was carried all the way to the US Supreme Court
And on December 12, 1938, the US Supreme Court in a 6-2 decision ordered the State of Missouri to admit Lloyd Gaines to the University of Missouri Law School
But if you travel down the road of America's past
You will discover that, despite the victory, Lloyd Gaines never enrolled at the University of Missouri
He never attended one class of law school and shockingly, he was never seen again
On the night of March 19, 1939, Lloyd Gaines mysteriously disappeared
Because America, again, was not ready for change
And despite the great victory, there was an even greater loss of a courageous young man
Lloyd Gaines never had the opportunity to fulfill his dream
He never enjoyed the opportunities to become the law student that America's highest court ordered or to become a lawyer
But even though he lacked those opportunities, Lloyd Gaines established his place in America's history
And even though his place may be well hidden
His lawsuit became one of the most important decisions to help defeat racial segregation in America

*And the decision of his case contributed significantly to the Brown versus Board of Education decision of 1954
So if you travel far enough down the road of America's past, you will discover the story of an unsolved mystery
But more importantly you will meet an American hero named Lloyd Lionel Gaines*

Langston's Words

Langston Hughes discovered the beauty of words growing up as a child
He realized as an adult the infinite possibilities that words could create through his life experiences and many travels
He learned that words were a source of power and strength
He saw that words could influence and change people even when the world was not quite ready for change
Langston's words introduced the world to a great poet, novelist, playwright, and social activist
But Langston was more than a poet and a writer
He was a man who cared for and loved his people and stressed that being Black was beautiful
He believed the black experience was definitely a part of the American experience
His words lifted up the Black race when there was not much lifting up going on for the Black race
His words painted and portrayed a realistic picture of America and of Blacks in America
His words revealed the joys, pain, achievements, and struggles of the black race during a time when there were few descriptions of what life was truly like for Blacks in America
His words addressed the subordinate conditions and status of Blacks in America
His words confronted the discrimination, inequality, racial stereotypes, and social conditions that were a way of life for Blacks in America
His words conquered hate, racism, and the indignities in a society where these had become the norm towards Blacks in America
Langston's words told the stories of the lives of black ordinary people
His words told it like it was and revealed the illusions that had falsely defined Black America and replaced those illusions with facts and the truth

His words dealt with the realities of being Black in America
His words were full of racial pride and cultural nationalism
His words were educational and informative and introduced the importance for Blacks to be racially conscious
His words addressed many issues that many people in America were afraid to address
Langston's words helped to describe America
Langston's words helped to describe his people
Langston's words helped to define the Harlem Renaissance
Langston's words made him an influential ambassador of creativity and expression
Langston's words helped to illuminate the artistic influence of poems and prose by many other Black authors
Langston's words were his personal testimony of his life
Langston's words were challenging, but un-attacking
Langston's words were deep, yet simplistic
Langston's words pierced the soul and touched the heart
Langston's words took people on journeys that caused them to examine themselves and of their position in the world
His words sometimes forced people to take a personal inventory of whom they were and where they needed to be
His words not only became an inspiration for other poets and writers, but his words united a world of people
Langston's words were not necessarily political, but they made political statements
Langston's words were not necessarily religious, but they were very spiritual
Langston's words made a statement during times when a statement needed to be made
Langston's words were a voice for those who did not have an avenue to replace their silence
Langston's words were the song lyrics to the rhythm of music that touched people of all races
Langston's words in his many books, plays, and poems helped him to receive worldwide acceptance as a writer whose work stressed racial awareness, culture and pride

Langston's words became a collection of work that was a symbol of literary relevance that became an inspiration for us all
Langston's words were an anthology of black culture and black experiences
Langston's words have traveled through time and they are just as respected today as they were when he first wrote them
Langston's words were pure
Langston's words were real
Langston's words were true
And Langston's words are still alive
Langston's words were his gift to the world
A precious and priceless gift from a true renaissance man
Langston's words

John Hope Franklin Believed in History

John Hope Franklin dedicated his life to American history
He taught and wrote of the history of Black people in this land called America
Born fifty years after the end of slavery in 1915
John Hope Franklin learned the importance of education from his parents
And for most of the ninety-four years of his life, he was committed to applying all of his knowledge to telling the history of Black people in America
The accurate and complete history of Black people in America
And during his long life, John Hope Franklin had come to know American history quite well
As an author, scholar, historian, teacher, as well as political and social activist
He broke down racial barriers with words as he researched the conscience of America
From slavery to freedom and beyond
His work changed the way Black history was viewed in America
He emphasized that Black history was American history
He refused to consider that Black history needed to be distinct
His work brought attention to what had become hidden secrets in American history
His work helped to emancipate the untold stories in American history
His work helped to create dialogue for racial reconciliation
His work paved the way for a brighter future in America
And his efforts and work left a trail for generations to follow
John Hope Franklin was committed to history
He believed history could change people
He believed history could change policy
He believed history could help change a nation
John Hope Franklin believed in history

*And despite facing discrimination and racism throughout his life
He remained committed and motivated to teaching and writing
the history of Black people in America
The American history of American people
From "Slavery to Freedom"
From a nightmare to a dream
From tragedy to triumph
John Hope Franklin believed in history
But he was more than a reporter of history, because he also contributed to making history
He received his PhD from Harvard University during a time when it was not easy for Blacks to get an education
He was the first Black historian to have a full-professorship at a white institution
He was the first Black to be appointed chair of the University of Chicago's history department
His research helped to build the case for the 1954 Brown versus Board of Education ruling that struck down the policy of "separate but equal"
He fought and marched for racial equality and against segregation in America
He was an advocate for equality and justice
He inspired his many students to thirst for truth, knowledge, and understanding
His numerous books and publications were a mirror to America
Revealing to America its many shames as well as its potential
He was a recipient of the NAACP's Spingarn Award and the nation's highest civilian honor, the Presidential Medal of Freedom
His more than 130 honorary degrees helped to define his legacy
John Hope Franklin believed in history and he was history
His contribution to America spanned more than six decades
And his work helped to show the value of the Black race to America's history
He used America's past to guide us into America's future
He challenged America to reach for its full potential as a nation*

And like the history he taught and wrote about
He helped to change America for the better
John Hope Franklin believed in history

Joe Louis and Jesse Owens Were American Heroes

They were African-American heroes when there were few national heroes for African- Americans
They became American heroes during a time when being a national hero was reserved for whites only
But Joe Louis and Jesse Owens were American heroes
They were true American heroes
Symbols of American devotion and pride
They were embraced by the world
Yet their own country offered them very little recognition or respect
Joe Louis and Jesse Owens were both born in segregated Alabama as sons of the Jim Crow South
Ironically, from their beginnings, they were introduced to the ugly side of America and to the disrespect they would face most of their lives
But that did not stop Joe Louis and Jesse Owens from becoming American heroes
It was not their dream to become American icons
But it became their destiny
And history reveals their legacy
The Thunder and the Lighting
The Brown Bomber and the Buckeye Bullet
The Heavyweight Boxing Champion
And the Olympic Track and Field Champion
The longest reigning heavyweight champion in boxing history
And the first American to win four Olympic gold medals in track and field
They defeated Nazi Germany during a time when Hitler was promoting racial superiority and the inferiority of Blacks
But as much as they were cheered and revered throughout the world

They suffered disrespect and pain from the nation they loved and represented
Joe Louis showed his American patriotism by twice donating his fight purse to military relief funds
After the country entered World War II, he enlisted and fought 96 exhibition fights to raise money for the military and to boost the nation's morale
His high profile helped to advance the efforts to desegregate the nation's military
And after all he had given to his country
Uncle Sam thanked him by saying he owed his country for what Joe Louis thought was patriotism
And doing what he thought he was supposed to do for his country
But this was how America treated an American hero
Jesse Owens was an eight time NCAA track and field champion at Ohio State University
But he never received an athletic scholarship there
He had to work part-time jobs to pay for his education
He was forced to stay at different hotels and eat in different restaurants from his teammates although he traveled with the team
But he still represented Ohio State University with pride
He represented his country in the 1936 Olympics and set world records
He represented his nation well and was an ambassador for America on the international stage
Yet the nation would not even honor him or say thank you to this American hero
And they even took away his ability to compete after he chose to capitalize off of his fame and status to help take care of his family
And again this was how America treated an American hero
After everything Joe Louis and Jesse Owens had done for their country

Their country treated them as though they were traitors and disowned them
Chasing them both mercilessly for back taxes until they both were bankrupt and financially broken
Causing both of these proud men to do things that no American hero should have had to do
Forcing them to work various odd jobs to support themselves
Even suffering the humiliations of racing animals, wrestling, and greeting at a casino to help pay their debts
There was no grace or mercy for them
The lives of these two American heroes, who won the hearts and minds of not just America, but of the world, were forever altered by the country they loved
Even though their own country treated them like they were second class citizens and not heroes
Joe Louis and Jesse Owens were, without doubt, American heroes

The Tuskegee Experiment - A Piece of History America Cannot Explain

Sometimes a piece of America's history is revealed that is just beyond belief and words truly cannot explain it
Sometimes America's past reveals hidden truths and seldom told stories that will demonstrate a different side of America
Sometimes a journey through America's past will reveal the sins of a nation
Sometimes an examination of America's historical facts will reveal the shame of America
A journey through America's history reveals the U.S. Public Health Service Study at Tuskegee
Better known as the Tuskegee Experiment or study
It is amazing how we can actually give this enough respect to even call it an experiment or study
Because it was more like medical injustice in the name of public health and science
A controversial study on syphilis without revealing to those participating in the study that they actually suffered from syphilis
A controversial study that refused to provide medical care or treatment to those participating in the study
This is a heartbreaking story about men who were promised a lie
The lie told by their government that they were being treated for "bad blood"
They were promised free medical care, free rides to appointments, free meals and free burial insurance
But what was the price for those freedoms?
They were never told the truth
These men were assured they were being treated for their illness by those that gave them a sense of hope for a cure for their unknown condition
A condition that was often debilitating and oftentimes fatal

This study represented a glimpse of hope for these unfortunate chosen men
Little did they know they were being used by their own government
They were transformed into human guinea pigs in the name of science
A government that was supposed to be a beacon of hope for these men instead became a master of deception to them
A so-called medical study on syphilis conducted between 1932 and 1972 in Tuskegee, Alabama turned nearly 400 poor African-American men into government slaves of scientific exploitation
Illiterate sharecroppers from one of the poorest counties in the country
Were mislead as their personal suffering turned into an unsympathetic plight with no one advocating for their rights
A governmental campaign of dehumanization and of right versus wrong
And even after penicillin was discovered and validated as a cure and effective treatment for the early stages of syphilis
For the next twenty-five years, the US government continued their study of shame and denied these men a treatment that could have either cured them or helped them in their suffering
America, the not so beautiful
Forty years of silence
Forty years of failing to treat these men like human beings
Forty years of total neglect and disrespect
Forty years of one of the most infamous biomedical crimes ever
And where was the bioethical outcry?
It took four decades until public health workers leaked this traumatic story of American history to the media
Bringing an end to a piece of America's history that America would rather forget
Forty years and twenty-eight men dead of syphilis
Forty years and one hundred men dead of syphilis related complications
Forty years and forty wives infected with syphilis

Forty years and nineteen children born with congenital syphilis
And as we take a moment to absorb this piece of American history
We realize that sometimes a piece of America's history is revealed that is just beyond belief and words truly cannot describe it
The Tuskegee Experiment is a piece of history America cannot explain

Vivien Thomas Was a Man with a Dream

If you would walk through the hallways of John Hopkins University School of Medicine
Portraits of some of America's greatest physicians adorn the walls
These portraits honor physicians who dedicated their lives to saving lives
Hanging on the walls with America's greatest minds of science and research is the portrait of Vivien Thomas
An unknown American hero, but a true American hero
Chances are, the name Vivien Thomas is not a name that is recognized when you hear it
Once you learn about his contributions to science and research you must ask why we do not know of the name Vivien Thomas
During a time when there was no place for a Black man in science and research
Vivien Thomas carved a place for himself
The Depression changed his dream of going to college and becoming a doctor
And he obtained a job working as a laboratory assistant for Dr. Alfred Blalock
Even with no education past high school, Vivien Thomas quickly excelled in performing complex and detailed surgical procedures, lab experiments, and data collection
He read and studied anatomy, chemistry and physiology textbooks to increase his knowledge
And he soon became indispensable to Dr. Blalock and his research
In 1944, Dr. Blalock was asked to correct a congenital heart defect known as "Blue Baby Syndrome" - a condition that claimed the lives of many children

Thomas was charged with the task of not only creating a blue baby-like condition in a dog, but then correcting the condition
He outlined the beginning of cardiac surgery and assisted in devising the procedures for the "Blue Baby" surgery that would save many lives
He accomplished all of this without a PhD, MD or even a college degree
When the first surgery was scheduled, he was not a member of the surgical team
Ironically, however, he became a part of the team that made medical history
Dr. Blalock required Vivien Thomas' assistance on that day and insisted that Thomas stand on a step stool behind him to coach him step by step through the procedure
You see, Thomas had mastered the procedure by performing the operation hundreds of times on dogs in the lab, while Dr. Blalock had only performed the procedure once
And even then, Blalock was Vivien Thomas' assistant
The success of the surgery made Dr. Blalock and the rest of the team famous
But Vivien Thomas remained an invisible man and his contributions remained hidden
And though he did not receive the recognition and respect he should have received
Vivien Thomas transcended the times as an educator, scientist, and as a man
He was a master surgeon who was unable to operate outside of his lab
He once made an incision so perfect it was described as "Something the Lord Made"
He helped to train many of America's leading surgeons who went on to head some of America's best hospitals
He was a pioneer and trailblazer in cardiac research
But it took more than 25 years before Thomas was given public recognition for his contributions to research and science
Twenty-five years for him to receive the respect he deserved

John Hopkins finally honored Vivien Thomas with his portrait being placed alongside the other medical greats and awarding him an Honorary Doctor of Laws degree
The dream that had eluded him most of his life was finally fulfilled
But although Vivien Thomas' name still remains unheard of to many, he was a man with a dream

The Tuskegee Airmen Soared Like Eagles

How do you tell a piece of American history?
When it's both a story of great achievement and of great adversity
How do you tell a piece of American history?
When it's a story of American patriotism and American pride
But it's also a story of American racism and discrimination
How do you tell a piece of American history?
When it's a story about men who helped to change a nation
But also a story about men who faced many challenges in the country they called home
How do you tell that piece of American history?
Well you tell the whole story!
You tell the story of how they flew into American history
And represented their country well
You tell how they were chosen and became the Tuskegee Airman
You tell how they trained, fought and died for America
And how they helped to protect America
You tell the story of almost a thousand trained pilots and over fifteen thousand ground personnel
And of their contribution towards world peace
You tell the story of how they came to be known as the Red Tail Angels
And how their achievements during World War II became well known
Fighting for America high in the skies
And fighting with courage and bravery
You tell the story of their fight for an opportunity to represent their country
And how they had to fight to gain respect from the nation they were fighting to protect
How do you tell that story?
You tell their story by telling their whole story

And not just bits and pieces of who they were, but what their role truly was
You tell the whole story of the Tuskegee Airmen
You tell of their over 1500 missions from 1941 to 1946
You tell how their journey took them to places such as Austria, Czechoslovakia, Germany, Hungary, Italy, Poland and Northern Africa
You tell how they desegregated the skies
You tell of their impressive record in protecting American Bombers
You tell of the many decorations awarded to them for their efforts, performance and valor
You tell how they helped to open the doors for change, opportunities and racial equality
You tell the whole story of the Tuskegee Airmen
You tell how they had to fight two wars
Fighting a war abroad and a war at home
Fighting a war abroad for world peace
And fighting a war at home for equality, freedom and justice
Despite the bigotry, hatred, humiliation and indignation
And though their fight to gain respect came with challenges
The Tuskegee Airmen accepted the challenges that came with showing they belonged
During a time when America was just as divided as the world that was at war
During a time when America was divided by race and segregation
The Tuskegee Airmen stood proud and strong
They knew the two worlds they lived in well, because race and segregation was a part of their lives everyday
Whether abroad or at home they had a battle to fight
But they persevered and their accomplishments helped to open many doors that once were closed to African-Americans
Their commitment, dedication and determination helped to change how African-Americans were viewed in America

How do you tell just a piece of American history when telling the story of some true American Heroes?
You tell the whole story of the Tuskegee Airmen place in American history
And how they soared like eagles and protected America in the skies

America Should Know the Name Dorie Miller

When you hear the name Dorie Miller
The response would probably be
Who?
But Dorie Miller was an American hero
An American hero whose name is seldom mentioned
An American hero who fought for America
An American hero who died for America
But an American hero whose name is unknown
Dorie Miller was stationed at Pearl Harbor
And as a mess attendant with the United States Navy on the battleship USS West Virginia
He responded above and beyond the call of duty on December 7, 1941
On a day which would live in infamy, yet his name would remain unknown
Dorie Miller went from a mess hall attendant to someone who carved his name into the history of America
When Japan invaded the United States and surprise attacked the American military forces of Pearl Harbor
Dorie Miller responded by defending America
During a time when African-Americans in the Navy could only served as mess attendants, stewards and cooks and were not trained to operate battleship weapons
Dorie Miller became a mighty man of valor
While his battleship was under fierce attack by the Japanese air force
Dorie Miller traveled back and forth to the bridge of the ship to assist the wounded
Even carrying his wounded captain to safety
And subsequently manning a 50 caliber anti-aircraft machine gun until he ran out of ammunition

Before Dorie Miller abandoned the damaged ship
He had shot down four Japanese planes
He did this on a weapon he had not been trained to use, nor had ever used before
On that day, Dorie Miller saved the lives of many
And for his extraordinary courage in battle, devotion to duty, and disregard for his own personal safety
Dorie Miller was awarded the Navy Cross
The second highest honor awarded by the Navy
The first for an African-American
But he was also entitled to the Purple Heart Medal; the American Defense Service Medal; the Fleet Clasp; the Asiatic-Pacific Campaign Medal; and the World War II Victory Medal.
But Dorie Miller failed to receive the recognition and respect he deserved
Dorie Miller later died during World War II when the ship he was stationed on sank in the Pacific
But he left a legacy that truly makes him an American hero
Dorie Miller died for America and America should know his name

The Few, the Proud, the Montford Point Marines

It is always interesting to find a piece of history that has been hidden and lost in the many chapters of American history
History that is often unrecognized and forgotten because of the disturbing truth of its reality
History that sometimes paints a picture of things in the past that America would rather forget
But America should not forget its history or its past
America should remember and learn from its past
And of the journey of the first African-American Marines who desegregated the United States Marine Corps and served their country well
Barely a footnote in America's history, the story of the Montford Point Marines was a lost story that should not have been forgotten
Their story was unlike the stories of the Buffalo Soldiers and Tuskegee Airman whose stories received at least some recognition
The story of the Montford Point Marines has been an example of selective amnesia by the United States Marine Corps and by America
But now it is a story that must be told
When President Franklin D. Roosevelt issued an Executive Order ending discrimination in the Armed Forces on June 25, 1941
The United States Marine Corps became the last military branch to accept African-Americans
From 1942 to 1949 nearly twenty-thousand African-Americans received their Marine Corps military training on a segregated military camp near Jacksonville, NC
Their commitment, courage, and strength gave them the determination to not fail and to excel and succeed as they fought to change the way the Marine Corps regarded all races

Though they were often treated like second class citizens and sometimes even treated worse
Though they were even given less respect than the captured German prisoners of war
And that blood sometimes called their names during WWII
They represented the Anchor, Eagle and Globe with pride
So their story must be told
It is a story that all Americans should know
It is a story that every Marine from private to general should know
But sadly it is a story that even some Marines have never heard
The story of how these brave men exemplified "Semper Fidelis" and were always faithful to their calling
The story of how these men rallied around the red, white and blue
And lived up to their motto
Because they were truly the few and the proud
In the face of adversity and their fight against discrimination, racism and the challenges of being stationed in the Jim Crow South
It was hard to distinguish if their war was overseas or in their own country
So their story, their journey, and their history must be respected
Receiving the Congressional Gold Medal, the highest civilian honor given by Congress is not enough
Much more respect is due to these men who served their country and the United States Marine Corps
The tragedy of their story being lost for the past seventy years must end
History must recognize those men that fought for freedom and equality in America's Armed Services
History must recognize those that helped to break the chains of this painful past
We must ensure the recognition of their story keeps the legacy of the Montford Point Marines alive

*And the recognition of their achievements and journey puts an exclamation point at the end of an era of irrelevance
And may we never forget the story of the Montford Point Marines
Because they were the few and the proud*

Dr. Benjamin Mays Wanted a Better America

Dr. Benjamin Mays wanted a better America
An America that was better than the post-slavery America his parents knew
An America that was better than the America that introduced to him as a child, the racial bigotry and intimidation that was a way of life in the South
An America that was better than the America of racial discrimination and segregation
Dr. Benjamin Mays wanted a better America
As a visionary, Dr. Benjamin Mays had a dream of a new and better America
An America that was better than the divided nation that had existed all of his life
An America that was better than the America he knew as President of Morehouse College
During a time when being a Negro President of an institution of higher learning did not exempt him from the racial challenges of America
Born to make a difference, Dr. Benjamin Mays was willing to fight for a better America
Being a son of former slaves from birth, he knew second class citizenship
He knew of the plight of the Negro and knew of the Negro's history in America's past
He also knew how much of the Negro's past was tragic beyond words
What is more, Dr. Benjamin Mays knew how to dream and he dreamed of a better America
An America that would boast equality, justice and social change for all of it citizens
An America that was Jim Crow free and no longer possessed an atmosphere of segregation

An America that was better than the America he had known all of his life
Dr. Benjamin Mays not only knew how to dream, but he taught others to dream
As an educator, minister, scholar, social activist and most of all, a mentor
He developed, taught, and influenced many students to dream and to fight for a better America
He shared his dream and vision for freedom, diversity and a different world
Dr. Benjamin Mays believed it must be birthed in the minds of all that the tragedy of life does not lie in not reaching your goals
But the tragedy of life lies in not having goals to reach
He believed it was not a calamity to die with dreams unfulfilled, but it was a calamity not to dream
He believed it was not a disgrace not to reach the stars, but it was a disgrace to have no stars to reach for
And he believed that dreaming and making dreams a reality would make the world a better place for all people
Dr. Benjamin Mays fought for a better America and for change in America
As an activist and advisor during the Civil Rights Movement, he organized peaceful protests
He confronted racism and the status quo of the South
He battled discrimination and challenged segregation in schooling, housing, and employment
As an outspoken critic of inequality and injustice and an advocate for higher education
He served as an advisor to several presidents of the United States
Playing an important role in the integration of America
He inspired Martin Luther King, Jr., Julian Bond, Lerone Bennett and many others to stand up for change
And the Morehouse mentor, with his words of wisdom, spiritual guidance, and intellectual leadership taught America about the power to dream and about being brave and courageous

He taught America about opening the window of opportunity and paving the road to equality
He believed one could transform being denied, disregarded, and disrespected into being accepted, acknowledged and respected
Dr. Benjamin Mays saw the future of America and his commitment to that dream and vision became his legacy

Jackie Robinson - A Real American Hero

Jackie Robinson was America's gift
During a time when America needed change and understanding
He was chosen to be the first
A pioneer who would break the color barrier in baseball
But that was not Jackie's only purpose
The world did not know the impact that Jackie would have on a society in need
A society in need of change
He not only changed baseball forever
But he helped to change America by opening up the doors for how we live today
Jackie was larger than baseball
He helped prepare America for something more than a game
He helped prepare America for what the future was bringing
Before Brown versus Board of Education, there was Jackie
Before Rosa Parks, there was Jackie
Before the Civil Rights Movement, there was Jackie
Before the marches and protests, there was Jackie
Before "I Have a Dream", there was Jackie
A great debt is owed to Jackie Robinson
Number forty-two gave Blacks the ability to dream
During a time when dreams did not always come true
He offered Blacks hope when there was not much to hope for
He inspired confidence in Blacks to believe that change could occur
He gave Blacks the courage to fight for change during a time when society was not quite ready to change
He became an example
Jackie endured hate, racism, and threats on his life

But he stood tall and kept his dignity
And did not lose sight of his mission and purpose
His courage and strength enabled him to hurdle the challenges he faced from a hostile society
A society that wanted to keep him from succeeding
Jackie was more than a great baseball player
Yes, he could run, hit, and catch a baseball
Yes, he is in the Hall of Fame for his adept skills as a baseball player
And for integrating the game
But beyond the baseball field, Jackie was a great man
He was a man of character and integrity
He was leader
He was a family man
He was a community and social activist
He was actively involved in the Civil Rights Movement
He was educated and served his country
Jackie Robinson is an American hero

Henrietta Lacks Lives!

If Henrietta Lacks were alive today
She would probably laugh if you told her she would save millions of lives around the world
And that she would have an important role in the search to find cures for cancer, leukemia, and Parkinson's disease
And that she would help in the development of medications for many illnesses and diseases
She would laugh even louder if you told her that she would also travel the world and beyond
If Henrietta Lacks were alive today
She would be convinced you were crazy if you told her she would live forever
And her contributions to science and research would start a medical revolution that would change the face of modern medicine and science
Yes! Henrietta Lacks would definitely think you were crazy
But surprisingly, Henrietta Lacks has helped to change the world
She was not a medical doctor, scientist, or researcher
But this ordinary woman who loved her family and life had an amazing impact on the world
Henrietta Lacks was a wife, a mother of five children, and a friend to many
A woman who migrated to Baltimore, Maryland with her husband from the tobacco fields of Southern Virginia seeking a better life
Seeking a life of dreams to be fulfilled during a Jim Crow era that did not always allow dreams for Blacks to be fulfilled
Who would believe this woman would one day give a lasting gift to the world?
On October 4, 1951, at the young age of thirty-one years, old Henrietta Lacks died of cervical cancer

She never would have imagined that succumbing to cancer would begin a life of immortality
Because unknown to her and her family and without their consent
While she received treatment in the colored ward of John Hopkins University Hospital
Cells were removed from her body
And for the first time ever after two decades of repeated failed attempts to create an immortal cell line for research
Henrietta Lacks' cells accomplished something that researchers had never seen before
They lived!
Not only did they live, they multiplied
With this discovery, the beginning of a new era in science was born
And Henrietta Lacks' contribution to science began
Her cells were named HeLa cells, but, unfortunately, her contributions to the world would remain unknown even to her family
Because after Henrietta Lacks' death and burial in an unmarked grave in southern Virginia
Her cells lived on and grew by the trillions in laboratories around the world
Being used in research and in the fight for cures of some of the world's most deadly diseases
But it was twenty-five years after her death before her family discovered her immortality
Twenty-five years before her family discovered that her cells were being mass produced, sold and used in research around the world
Her cells were even present on some of the first NASA space missions
They never knew her cells were still alive and had become a billion dollar industry
They never received a penny from the exploitation of her immortality

The HeLa Cells are known by researchers and science students around the world
But Henrietta Lacks has received very little recognition for her contributions to science
And few in science even recognize her name although science has received so much from her immortal cells
So let the truth be told regarding the contributions and historical meaning of the HeLa Cells
All of those cells belong to Henrietta Lacks
The HeLa cells changed the scientific world and the world will never be the same because Henrietta Lacks lives!

How Do You Name the Black Experience? (You Can't!)

The slaughter of six million Jews by Nazi Germany is called the Holocaust
The mass murder of millions of people in Bosnia, Cambodia, Rwanda and Sudan is called Genocide
The forty-six year system of legal racial segregation and oppression in South Africa was called Apartheid
But there is no name for the African-American experience in America
And for the treatment of African-American people and the atrocities against them
From their homeland in Africa to Jamestown, Virginia in 1619 to a long fought fight for true freedom
Through the Middle Passage, slavery, post reconstruction, segregation and the disfranchisement of a people
The historical experience of the African-American people has never been named or fully defined
How can you name and define people being stolen from the land they called home only to have their names and identity taken?
How can you name and define a lost culture and a stolen legacy?
How can you name and define the mental, physical, and psychological abuse that has cursed African-American people from generation to generation?
There is no name to describe this crime against humanity and against American people
One word cannot describe the impact of the acts that are the shame of a nation
America - the nation of dreams and freedom
But also the nation where dreams have been taken away and replaced with nightmares of freedom lost

A legacy of Africans falling victim to the second class citizenship that was awaiting them upon their arrival to America
Welcome to America!
And welcome to a legacy that was manifested in slavery
The scars from the bullwhip of the slave masters and the branding of slaves as property
The mental scars haunting the slave women raped and the families broken up and destroyed by the cruelties of slavery
The bravery of the many slaves who risked their lives and chanced the consequences of being captured as a runaway while chasing the North Star for freedom
Just for the chance to feel freedom and to feel human
How can you provide a name for being labeled and treated as less than a human being?
From the emancipation of slavery to a return to the subordinate status under slavery that came with Post-Reconstruction
And that is what the Jim Crow era introduced to America with the racial discrimination, divide and segregation laws that came with that period in American history
Being in America, but not being treated like Americans had become the American way
How can you name and define the experience of a people who were not allowed to vote without some form of opposition
Having to take literacy tests, paying poll taxes and being the victims of restrictive covenants was the required law in many places for African-Americans
How can you name and define having to fight for equality and justice?
Remembering Plessy versus Ferguson and the Supreme Court mandated decision of "separate but equal"
But even with the court's decision, America was still separate and still unequal
Remembering the racial terrorism that the fight for freedom, justice, and equality brought

And of the lynching, violence, murders, cross burnings, bombings and race riots that created an atmosphere of anxiety, fear and intimidation
Remembering the journey of the many who fought and died for change and to be fully accepted and embraced by America
How can you name and define the breaking of the spirit of a people?
When they have suffered from racial hatred, inequality and mass racial disparities
How do you name and define the African-American experience in America?
When they as a people have been on the other side of America's freedom
How do you name and define the Black experience?
You can't!

Twenty-eight Days

Only twenty-eight days
To recognize the history of Black people in America
Twenty-eight days
Twenty-eight days to focus on a history that is over four hundred years old
A history of great people
A history of great achievements
A history of great gains
A history of great struggles
A history of pain and suffering
Only twenty-eight days
To focus on Black history
American history and the history of people who helped to define America
People who helped to build America!
People who fought for America!
People who died for America!
A history that is far more worthy than twenty-eight days
From slavery to a national holiday for a King
The history of Black people is American history
Martin, Malcolm, Marcus and Medgar
Birmingham, Jackson, Montgomery and Selma
Jazz, gospel, blues, rhythm & blues, and hip-hop
Black people have impacted America
Black people's history is real and very strong
A history, if you recognized it every day for a year
You would still have much history left over
So twenty-eight days is just not enough time
To recognize and remember
The legacies of A. Phillip Randolph, W.E.B. Du Bois, Ida B. Wells, and Sojourner Truth
Twenty-eight days is not enough time
To recognize and remember

The scientific achievements of Dr. Ben Carson, Dr. Charles Drew, and Dr. Daniel Hale Williams
Twenty-eight days is not enough time
To recognize and remember
The lives of Rosa Parks, Matthew Henson, and Ed Bradley
Twenty-eight days is not enough time
To recognize and remember
The protests of Stokely Carmichael, Bob Moses, Diane Nash, and Fannie Lou Hamer
Twenty-eight days is not enough time
To recognize and remember
The writings of James Baldwin, Ralph Ellison, and Richard Wright
Twenty-eight days is not enough time
To recognize and remember
The March on Washington, the Freedom Riders, and the Black Panther Party
Twenty-eight days is not enough time
To recognize and remember
The life of Emmitt Till
Twenty-eight days is just not enough time to recognize and remember Black people in America
The story of their journey
Twenty-eight days is not enough time
To recognize and remember fully the history of Black people in America
So America, you owe Black history three hundred and thirty seven more days

Before There Was a Civil Rights Movement, There Was Vernon Johns

When you trace the roots of the Civil Rights Movement
History will reveal that before there was a movement
There was a man named Vernon Johns
Before there was Rosa Parks or Dr. Martin Luther King
There was a man named Vernon Johns
Before there were marches and protests throughout the South
There was a man named Vernon Johns
He was a pioneer
A forgotten hero
A man whose bravery and courage laid the groundwork for a movement that changed America
A look into America's past
Will confirm Vernon Johns should be more than just a footnote in the history and journey of Blacks in America
But unfortunately, he and his legacy are quite unknown
Vernon Johns strongly opposed segregation and he cared about the plight of Black people
He fought against the Jim Crow laws of the South
As pastor and predecessor to Dr. King at the Dexter Avenue Baptist Church in Montgomery, Alabama his fiery messages challenged the oppressed and the oppressor
He spoke out against injustice and other racial issues
And was critical of Blacks for ignoring them
Vernon Johns was a man ahead of his time in the fight for the civil and human rights of Blacks in the South
He helped to lay the framework for a mass movement that would challenge racial injustice, inequality and the wrongs of America
Vernon Johns was not afraid to take a stance
Several years before the Montgomery bus boycotts, he refused to move to the back of the bus, demanding his fare back and receiving it

He summoned Black passengers to walk and to protest riding the buses
He was bold enough to order food in an all-white restaurant
He spoke out publicly in opposition to the violent acts against Blacks in the south
He persuaded Black women to bring charges in court against White rapists
And even though there were no convictions, it was a major achievement for these cases to reach the courts
He believed that Blacks should support each other economically
He encouraged Blacks to sell goods instead of buying goods from whites who did not respect their patronage
And he did all of this before Rosa refused to get out of her seat
His sermons spoke of equality for Blacks, economic independence and racial uplift
He preached that segregation would continue unless it was challenged and defeated
And he encouraged Blacks to stand up and fight
Vernon Johns used to say that if you see a good fight then you need to get in it
He believed in change and he did his part, but the time was not right
Instead, his efforts were lessons that laid the foundation for change
Because before there was a Civil Rights Movement, there was Vernon Johns

Sometimes You Only Need to Say the Name, Thurgood Marshall

Sometimes you only need to say the name
And the name will say it all
Totally defining a person
Breaking down who they were, what they stood for, and even describing their legacy
Sometimes you only need to hear the name
And the name alone will provide a biography and take you on a historical journey
Sometimes you only need to say the name
And nothing else needs to be said
All that is needed is the mere mention of the name
And that alone provides everything that is needed to understand the impact of that life
Thurgood Marshall had one of those names
A name that demanded honor and respect
A name that tells of the making of a Supreme Court Justice
A name that when mentioned tells the story of a difference-maker in American history
Sometimes you only need to say the name
And you immediately identify the name with how he was a warrior for equality, freedom and justice
You immediately identify the name with the voice for the voiceless in the battle for equality
You immediately identify the name with the work of one of the architects that helped to change the landscape of American society forever
Sometimes you only need to say the name
And you will understand the high calling of the individual
And Thurgood Marshall had a high calling
A fighter for and a protector of the integrity of the Constitution
Thurgood Marshall believed in the Constitution of America

He believed the Constitution was the supreme law of the land and that this precious document was the foundation of America
He believed the Constitution was the legal authority that defined America
And he would dedicate his life to using the Constitution to make America what America was founded to be
Sometimes you only need to say the name
And you would know that Thurgood Marshall believed in change
He believed that America was for all Americans
He believed there was no place for the legal doctrine called "Separate but Equal"
Nor was there a place for discrimination or the legacy of Jim Crow laws in America
The name will not only remind you of the Brown versus the Board of Education decision of 1954
But of the numerous other landmark cases that helped to shape America and put an end to legal segregation in America
It will remind you of the twenty-nine out of thirty-two cases he argued and won before the Supreme Court challenging discrimination in education, housing, voting, and transportation
Sometimes you only need to say the name
And it will remind you of a man that not only fought for the rights of African- Americans
But of a man who fought for the rights of all Americans
The name Thurgood Marshall is more than a story of a great lawyer and Supreme Court judge
The name Thurgood Marshall is more than a story of some legal and moral victories
The name Thurgood Marshall reminds America of the man whose impact helped to change America forever

One Name Truly Stand Out - Barbara Johns

A journey through African-American history will reveal many names in its history
And though many of the names are well known
There are many names that would cause you to ask, "Who?"
Many individuals whose place in history should have been bookmarked
Have become historical mysteries
Their names and stories in history have become unknown to most
You may be able to hide the past, but you can never destroy the past
Nor the legacies of those who have lived forever in the many hidden chapters of American history
When you look deep into the history and journey of African-Americans
One name will truly stand out
And it is the name of Barbara Johns
A name in African-American history that introduced African-American children to the fight for equality
A name that confronted segregation and America's racial divide
A name that had recognized the reality of the African-American's experience and made a commitment to change and eradicate that reality
A name of an unsung hero
At the age of sixteen years old, Barbara Johns had become frustrated and tired of living in a world that was not equal
She was frustrated and tired of being treated as if her education did not matter in Prince Edward County, Virginia
She was frustrated and tired of the separate and unequal education she was receiving at Robert R. Moton High School in Farmville, Virginia

She was frustrated and tired of attending the overcrowded dilapidated school that was in dire need of repairs and renovations
She was frustrated and tired of the school's hand-me-down resources and lack of quality school supplies
She was frustrated and tired of white children attending new schools with new books while Black children attended schools with no heat and few books
But Barbara Johns - whose uncle was the outspoken activist for civil rights, the Reverend Vernon Johns - made up her mind to do something
And guided by her conscience and by what she knew was right Barbara Johns came up with a plan that would help destroy separate and unequal education across America
And on April 23, 1951 the young Barbara Johns propelled her classmates of over four hundred fifty students into action
She led the entire student body of her high school on a protest and strike for integration and equal education
They marched out of school and to the county courthouse
Where they shared their concerns about how tough it was to learn under substandard conditions and with a lack of quality educational resources
As the strike continued, the persistent Barbara Johns and community leaders sought the legal counsel of the NAACP
And with the NAACP's support, they legally challenged the segregated educational system of Prince Edward County
With a promise of legal action against the school system from the NAACP
Barbara Johns and her classmates agreed to return to school
On May 23, 1951, lawyers for the NAACP filed suit on behalf of the students against the School Board of Prince Edward County to integrate the schools
After defeats in the state court and the US District Court, their case made its way all the way to the US Supreme Court
And as one of four cases that made up the famous Brown versus Board of Education case of 1954

The Supreme Court officially declared that racial segregation in public schools was unconstitutional
And although the courageous actions and efforts of Barbara Johns did eventually bring equality and justice to African-Americans throughout the state of Virginia
The fight she initiated also caused a lot of fears, pain and suffering
Because her family feared for her life and safety after their home was burned down and a cross burned in their yard, she was sent to another state to live with relatives
And many in their community were denied credit and work because of this fight for what was right
Even after the Supreme Court decision, Virginia lawmakers passed laws allowing the state to close public schools in defiance of federally mandated integration
Choosing to close schools rather than integrate resulted in many white children to attending private tuition free schools
While denying and eliminating African-American children an opportunity for a free public education
It was not until 1964 - five years later - that federal courts were finally able to overturn the efforts of the state of Virginia and proclaim them unconstitutional
Those that were once denied, disregarded, and disrespected
Now entered through the window of opportunity for a free and equal education
And of a brighter future
The bravery and efforts of one young lady set in motion events that would help to change an entire nation
And when you look deep into the history and journey of African-Americans
One name will truly stand out
And it is the name of Barbara Johns

A Day that Changed America Forever (Brown versus Board of Education of Topeka)

A Day that changed America
May 17, 1954 was a day that changed America forever
A decision on five cases combined by the Supreme Court
Under the heading of Brown versus Board of Education of Topeka
Challenged the institution of America
Belton versus Gebhart of Delaware
Briggs versus Elliot of South Carolina
Davis versus County School Board of Prince Edwards County of Virginia
Bolling versus Melvin Sharpe of Washington, DC
And the Brown cases together comprised a case that had a far greater impact on America than any other court case in America's history
The Brown decision made a statement
And that statement was separate could not mean equal in America any longer
A landmark, unanimous decision by a Supreme Court that was brave enough to challenge the status quo and change America during a time when America was resistant to change
The Plessy versus Ferguson decision for almost sixty years was the law of the land
And it ruled separate but equal was the American way, even though separate never came close to being equal in America for African-Americans
The Brown decision established a new doctrine
And that doctrine was that Plessy versus Ferguson was both unconstitutional and unacceptable

America with a history of slavery
A history of labeling African-Americans as less than a human
A history of denying human rights and equality to people who helped build America
Was due for a makeover
The Brown decision launched the beginning of change
Attacking a racial divide that had existed since America's beginning
The Brown decision was not the first legal challenge to "separate but equal"
The Supreme Court ordered that desegregation occur "with all deliberate speed"
Which meant, "America you take your good old time desegregating because we did not put a time frame on this decision"
But the Brown decision was the victory that helped launch a movement, because the Brown decision provided African-Americans with the courage to start a Civil Rights Movement
And even with massive resistance from those that preferred America just the way it was
The Brown decision was a stepping stone to the historic movement that changed America
The decision not only desegregated the public schools, but it set a precedent to desegregate all public places
The Brown decision was more than the case's namesake-Oliver Brown and his daughter Linda Brown
The Brown decision was more than Thurgood Marshall and the other crusaders who fought the case
The decision was about America and what America was supposed to be
And even with massive resistance from those that preferred America just the way it was
And the Supreme Court ordering that desegregation occur "with all deliberate speed"

*Which meant, America you take your good old time
desegregating because we did not put a time frame on this
decision
The Brown decision was about America's past and about
America's future
And it changed America forever*

Medgar Evers and a New Day

All Medgar wanted was a new day
A day when blacks in Mississippi were able to live as freely as whites in Mississippi
A day when there would be liberty, equality, and justice for all in Mississippi
A day when the nation would not be divided by the notion that one race was inferior to another
All Medgar wanted was a new day
A day when racism, discrimination, and prejudice would no longer exist
A day when Black Mississippians would not have to worry about being the next Emmitt Till
A day when victims of hate crimes and lynching would be acts no more
All Medgar wanted was a new day
A day when Mississippi would be a different place for his children than it was for him
A day when there would be no need to fight for civil and human rights
A day when there would be no need for demonstrations and protests
All Medgar wanted was a new day
A day when Blacks in Mississippi could register to vote and cast their votes without fear
A day when schools, stores, and restaurants would be welcome to all
A day when "white only" signs would be a part of Mississippi's past
All Medgar wanted was a new day
A day when Mississippi would be better known for the beauty of its southern scenery than for its efforts to hold on to the old ways of the South

A day when Mississippi would not wave the confederate flag as a symbol of Mississippi pride
A day when great race relations would be a symbol of the state of Mississippi
All Medgar wanted was a new day
A day when blacks would no longer feel the scars of Jim Crow laws and racial segregation
A day when Blacks were no longer treated like second class citizens
A day when everyone in Mississippi would have government representation
All Medgar wanted was a new day
A day when there would be no more shattered dreams
A day when no one would be haunted by America's shameful past
A day when blacks in Mississippi would no longer have to fight for justice
All Medgar wanted was a new day
A day when race would not matter
A day when there would be no need for the NAACP
A day when there would be no Ku Klux Klan, White Citizens Council, or Byron de la Beckwith
All Medgar wanted was a new day
And though he never saw that day appear
Medgar Evers helped to move America towards a new day
Medgar dreamed of a new day
Medgar fought for a new day
And Medgar died for a new day
Helping America to open the door for change
Helping America to reach from its past to grab a better future
Helping America to understand that true democracy required a new America and a change in America
And though they killed the dreamer, they were unable to the kill the dream
Or the beginning of a new day

Their Names Are Not Famous
(The Little Rock Nine)

Their names are not famous
But Melba Pattillo Beals, Minnijean Brown, Elizabeth Eckford,
Ernest Green, Gloria Ray Karlmark, Carlotta Walls LaNier,
Thelma Mothershed, Terrence Roberts, and Jefferson Thomas
Changed America
They were not looking to make history
But their courage bestowed upon them a chapter in American history
Known as the Little Rock Nine
They were teenagers whose bravery changed America forever
All they desired was an education
A good education
But they were called to change a system of inequality
To change an institution of segregation at Central High School in Little Rock, Arkansas
To change the educational landscape of America
To uphold the law
They were called to show America it was time to end separate and what was called equal
They were called to make a change
They were committed to what they were called to do and determined to get a decent education
On a September day in 1957, these Black students set off on their mission to desegregate Central High School
To obtain the education they deserved
Yes! They experienced fear and the feeling of not knowing what they were about to encounter
But they did not shy away from the goal they set out to achieve
On that September day
They attempted to enter their new school, but confronted by a mob of angry protesters

And blocked by the state's national guards on orders from the governor to deny their entrance
They were turned away
But they returned
Only to confront racism
And more abuse and rejection
Their historic act forced President Eisenhower to send federal troops to uphold integration and protect these nine brave students
And after unrelenting efforts and the support of the federal government their goal was achieved
And even though the image of their attempts to enter Central High School still retains its power
These unknown nine students became the face of a movement
They became part of the legacy of the Civil Rights Movement and they paved the way for change in America

When I Think of the History of Black People in America

When I think of the history of Black people in America
I think of the journey of Black people
I think of the Black experience
And the impact Blacks have had on America and the impact America has had on Blacks
I think of the contributions, legacy, and the strength of Black people
But I also think of the struggles of Black people
And what Black people have endured since coming to America
When I think of the history of Black people in America
I think of America the beautiful
But I also think of America the not so beautiful
I think of the people that endured a journey unlike any other people in America's history
I think of the people who built America, fought for America, and died for America
But these same people were enslaved in America
These same people were the victims of racism, discrimination, and hate crimes in America
These same people were persecuted and suffered greatly in America
When I think of the history of Black people in America
I think about the fight for freedom
And how freedom came with a cost
I think about the fight for equality
And how equality had not been free
I think about the price that was paid for freedom and equality
And how I am thankful for people who fought for that freedom and equality
I think of the opening words of the Constitution
"We the people of the United States, in order to form a more perfect union"

And how to this day we have not been a part of any perfect union
When I think of the history of Black people in America
I think beyond February
I think of history that deserves to be recognized every day and not just for a month
I think of history that should be a part of every school's curriculum
I think about a history that connects us to the present
No matter how brutally honest that history may be, because it is America's history
When I think of the history of Black people in America
I think of the Constitution
And I think of how Blacks had to fight to be recognized in this document
I think of the Civil Rights and Voting Rights Acts
I think of how Blacks needed to have legislation to secure the rights as citizens in this country
And of all of the laws that were established to keep Black people down and oppressed
When I think of the history of Black people in America
I think of the unrecognized warriors for freedom
I think of those people who sang for freedom, justice, and equality
I think of those people who appealed to the conscience of the nation and started movements for change from the Abolitionist Movement to the Civil Rights Movement
But I also think of the legacy of racism and injustice towards Blacks in America
When I think of the history of Black people in America I think of American history

The Greensboro Four

In 1776, Thomas Jefferson and America's founding fathers signed the United States Declaration of Independence
They declared, "We hold these truths self-evident, that all men are created equal, that they are endowed by their Creator with certain unalienable rights, that among these are Life, Liberty and the Pursuit of Happiness"

But let the truth be told
These words were not always accurate in the practices of America and had become the Contradiction of the complexities of America
America could not always declare that they practiced what they preached
And though America preached that all men were created equal, the reality was far from the truth
Deciphering through America's history and understanding the legacy of America's deep past will reveal images from America's journey that will forever retain its power
The images of a Black America and a white America
And the stark differences of being Black and being white in America
The images of how racial discrimination and the ugliness of Jim Crow was about as American as apple pie
The images of "colored only" signs and sitting in the back of buses
The images that have shown the realities of America's not so distant past
But there was also an image on February 1, 1960
When Joseph McNeil, Franklin McCain, David Richmond, and Ezell Blair, Jr. decided to sit down and create an image that would be forever etched in the minds of Americans
An image of fighting for equality
An image of fighting for justice
An image that cried, "Enough is enough!"

The Greensboro Four, as they came to be known, helped to initiate the sit-in movement
The four North Carolina A & T students took a seat for what was morally right
And by taking a seat at the counter of a Woolworth lunch counter
They took a stand against segregation and what was wrong in America
They helped to change America forever
Their historical act helped to start a movement in the South that challenged a democracy that was unequal and unjust
They helped to eradicate the color-line in education, employment, housing, and recreation
They created a pathway to understanding and an image of how far America has come as a nation
They helped America realize that everyone could have and live an American Dream
And that "All men are created equal"
Four young men took their seat for what was right and they helped to make America a better place

Malcolm X

From Malcolm Little
To Detroit Red
To Malcolm X
To El-Hajj Malik El-Shabazz
From a street hustler
To a street messenger
Malcolm X was a complex man
But more than anything
Malcolm X was a man
A man who would not compromise his beliefs or his mission
A man who was not afraid to stand up against inequality and racism
As a minister and national spokesman for the Nation of Islam
Malcolm became the voice that was feared
With a message of Black Nationalism
He instilled pride in his people
And who taught "Where there is no vision, the people perish"
A true revolutionary
Malcolm did not believe in turning the other cheek to the American violence against Blacks
But he believed Black people should protect themselves by "Any Means Necessary"
He was the embodiment of Black Power
His speeches influenced many people such as Stokely Carmichael, H. Rap Brown, and the Black Panther Party
After his break with the Nation of Islam, Malcolm continued to evolve and transform as a man, but he remained the same charismatic and fiery fighter for his people
He was a model for American Black liberation
He believed in the emancipation of his people
He associated black people's struggle in America with the struggle of African people around the world
He believed the Black American's fight was bigger than a fight for their civil rights

But should be a fight for their God-given human rights
Malcolm believed in raising the consciousness of Black people
But unfortunately, America struggled to understand Malcolm
And often his legacy and his place in history are minimized
The man who taught that we needed to shake the chains of slavery once and for all is often forgotten in American history
The man whose life and ideas continue to inspire and motivate generations long after the voice was silenced
Every February we offer very little recognition and respect to Malcolm X
Malcolm fought and died for the people he loved
And his place in history cannot be denied
You see Malcolm had a dream as well, and his dream was not much different from Dr. Martin Luther King's dream or the American dream
Malcolm wanted his people to be all they could be and to truly be able to experience this so-called American dream
Without being the victims of hate, racism, and injustice
Malcolm wanted his people to live freely and to be respected in America

Taking a Stance Meant Taking a Seat

For some of America's people, taking a stance meant taking a seat
For many Blacks all they wanted was equality and justice in the country they called home
But in this America that defined and preached democracy and freedom to the world
America struggled to fully embrace democracy and freedom on its own soil
During a time when discrimination, racism, and the ills of Jim Crow laws were alive and active in America
There were a few people that were bold, brave, and courageous enough to take that stance
To accept the status quo was no longer an option for them
The memories of their people's past experiences made them say, "Enough was enough."
Accepting the treatment or doing nothing was no longer acceptable
They did not choose to be a part of history, but they became a part of America's history
And though many of their names and stories are unknown and are well-hidden in history
The facts are that they quietly made a statement for change in America
And sometimes taking a stance meant refusing to get up or just sitting down
We often hear the story of Rosa Parks
And how her actions help to launch the Civil Rights Movement
Who in 1956 was arrested after refusing to give up her seat and move to the back of a city bus in Montgomery, Alabama
But we do not hear of how Ida B. Wells challenged segregation decades before Rosa Parks
And how in 1884 she was physically removed from a train after refusing to give up her seat

History books do not tell the story of Irene Morgan, who in 1944 was arrested for refusing to give up her seat to a white passenger while travelling on a Greyhound bus in Virginia
And how her actions led to a landmark Supreme Court decision that paved the way for future civil right court victories
We do not hear the stories of Claudette Colvin and Vernon Johns Who both refused to give up their seats to whites and were forced off buses in the same city that Rosa Parks took her seat
For some of America's people, taking a stance meant taking a seat
We often hear the story of the four North Carolina A & T students that staged a sit-in protest in 1960 to desegregate a white-only lunch counter in Greensboro, NC
But we do not hear the stories of at least 15 other sit-in demonstrations from 1943 to 1960
We do not hear the stories of how in 1958 Black college students in Tennessee staged sit-ins to desegregate the lunch counters in two Nashville, Tennessee department stores
Or how students from Wiley and Bishop Colleges in 1958 organized the first sit-in protests in Texas
Their actions did not capture the attention of the world
But their actions did have an impact on America
For some of America's people, taking a stance meant taking a seat
In 1961, busloads of Freedom Riders waged a campaign testing the Supreme Court's ruling that segregated seating on interstate buses and trains was unconstitutional
More than 300 Freedom Riders traveled through the South in an effort to integrate the bus terminals and even though their protest rides were met with arrests, opposition and violence
Their actions helped to desegregate and change America
So we must remember the many people that helped to make America what it is today
And let us remember that some people in America believed that taking a stance meant taking a seat

Dorothy I. Height - The Godmother of the Civil Rights Movement

As you turn the pages of American history
You will discover a woman known as the Godmother of the Civil Rights Movement
You will discover a woman who spoke out against segregation
You will discover a woman who fought for equality in America
You will discover a woman who in 1963 marched in Washington, DC and stood on the steps of the Lincoln Memorial with Dr. Martin Luther King, Jr.
Because she believed that taking a stance for what was right would lead to a better tomorrow
As you turn the pages of American history, you will discover Dr. Dorothy I. Height
A woman who wore her hats in the semblance of crowns
A woman who carried herself with the eloquence and regality of a queen
A woman who shined with the self-confidence and self-respect of a woman who knew her calling
And Dr. Dorothy I. Height was a woman who knew her calling
As you turn the pages of American history
You will discover the story of a woman who knew that freedom and equality was not free
You will discover a woman who in her tireless efforts, fought for the rights of African-Americans, women, the poor, and other minorities
You will discover a woman that helped to break the chains that held America from true democracy
You will discover a woman who advised presidents and was respected around the world
You will discover a woman who was a humanitarian, a historian, a mentor, and a visionary

You will discover a woman who was a crusader for freedom and justice
Dr. Dorothy I. Height was a woman who stood for what was right
She was a woman who spent her long life fighting for equality, justice, and opportunity
She was the bridge that connected the African-American's past to the present
She painted the clear picture of what the future of America could be if America would only Open wide the gates of equality, justice, and opportunities for all people
And this is what Dr. Dorothy I. Height dedicated her life towards obtaining
She was not so concerned about getting credit or recognition
She was concerned about change and the causes that could help change America for the better
Her commitment was seen in leading the National Council of Negro Women for more than four decades
Her commitment was seen in fighting segregation in the South
Her commitment was seen in organizing a program called "Wednesdays in Mississippi,"
A program that helped to improve race relations in the South by bringing African-American and white women together to create a dialogue of respect and understanding
Her commitment was seen in fighting for voting rights for African-Americans
Her commitment was seen in fighting for equal employment opportunities for African-Americans
Her commitment was seen in being a voice for all women in America
And as you turn the pages of American history you will find Dr. Dorothy I. Height
An American heroine who helped to change the course of American history

The Civil Rights Movement Changed America

The period between 1954 and 1968 is considered one of the greatest periods of America's history
A period in time that had an impact on America like no other time during its history
A period that said, "No more!"
And that it was time for America to change or for America to be changed
America, a nation that was established because people wanted their freedom
A nation that preached what it stood for through its founding fathers and great leaders
And through its "Constitution" and "Declaration of Independence"
But America with a history from its beginning of not practicing what it preached
Because America did not always practice freedom, justice and liberty
America practiced disfranchisement, exploitation, segregation and violence towards African- Americans and this was after they had already endured slavery
America's form of "Apartheid" painted a not so pretty picture of America
And it took a movement to change America
The Civil Rights Movement was born because America needed to change
The Civil Rights Movement was bigger than one person, a protest or a legal victory
The Civil Rights Movement was about the bravery and courage of many people
People who were willing to fight for equality, justice and for what the American way was supposed to be

People who were willing to fight for freedom and the desegregation of America
People who were willing to fight so they and those coming behind them could say they were an American and were proud to be an American
The Civil Rights Movement was about the justification of African-American people
And their rights as citizens and human beings in America
The Civil Rights Movement was about the unification of America's people coming together to make America a better place for all people
The movement with it strategies of protests, non-violent resistance and legal actions led to boycotts, sit-ins, voter registrations, and protest marches throughout the South
The movement gave African-Americans the ammunition to gain victories for change in such places as Birmingham, Greensboro, Jackson, Montgomery and Selma
The movement led to court victories and legislation being passed that gave equal rights not only to African-Americans, but to all Americans
Because the legacy of the Civil Rights Movement was not just about African-Americans it was about America and all of America's people
The efforts of the NAACP, CORE, SCLC and SNCC were not in vain
The contributions of people like James Farmer, Ralph Abernathy, Ella Baker and Fannie Lou Hamer was not in vain
The deaths of Martin Luther King, Jr., Medgar Evers and countless others who died for change was not in vain
Their lives were not lost in vain
The Freedom Riders, Freedom Summer and the March on Washington
Did not define the Civil Rights Movement
The contributions, efforts and sacrifices of many and what we see today define the legacy of the Civil Rights Movement

When America was long overdue for a change the Civil Rights Movement changed America

No Ordinary People

The journey of African-American people tells a story
The story of an American journey like no other
A journey with almost four hundred years of history
A journey that has gone from slavery to the White House
The journey of African-American people reveals one extraordinary fact
They are no ordinary people
As history speaks
The legacy of a people is revealed
Reaching out from the past on this journey to the present reveals an amazing story
From the slave ships leaving the shores of Africa
To an African-American being elected as the 44th President of the United States of America
African-Americans are no ordinary people
From being branded like livestock and abused as slaves
To becoming corporate CEO's and university presidents
African-Americans are no ordinary people
From a shameful part of America's past and of an American nightmare
To American dreams becoming reality
African-Americans are no ordinary people
As we past-forward
And examine the dreams that have been deferred from generation to generation
Dreams of change
Dreams of hope
Dreams of freedom
Dreams of a better tomorrow
No ordinary people could keep their eyes on the prize while enduring a historical past that many would rather forget
A past of racial discrimination and political divide
A past that suggested that all men were not created equal

A past that showed color affects the outcome of justice in America
But no ordinary people could follow this path to freedom
Down a trail filled with obstacles from a systematic campaign of dehumanization
Attacking a race of people physically, psychologically, and culturally
African-Americans are no ordinary people
From an invisible history to not being able to deny their history
From being submerged as a people to emerging as a people
Only an extraordinary people could continue their journey and to "Lift Every Voice and Sing"
Trusting in God through their times of despair while following a path that was different than any other group of people's journey in America's history
Only an extraordinary people
Could bear the scars of oppression and still rise
Only an extraordinary people
Could pave the way to a brighter tomorrow
While remembering the realities of the past
African-Americans are no ordinary people

Forty-five years, Nine Months and Thirteen Days

After forty-five years, nine months and thirteen days
I guess we can say justice has been served
Or can we?
Because Alabama state trooper James Fowler at the age of seventy-seven finally went to jail on December 1, 2010 for the murder of Jimmie Lee Jackson
And through a plea bargain agreement gave him only a six month sentence
Justice had finally arrived and an unpunished killing was unpunished no more
The wait for justice was over and in the end justice was not denied
But was it really justice and was justice truly served
After forty-five years, nine months and thirteen days
The cold case is cold no more
But sadly, the name Jimmie Lee Jackson is still unknown to many
One cannot find the name or story in many history books
The name is very seldom commemorated during Black History Month
But the name Jimmie Lee Jackson is an important name in Black History
Jimmie Lee Jackson did not die in vain, but he died fighting for change
He knew well of the dangers of standing tall for what was right in a part of the country where the confederate flag was waved proudly
He knew in Marion, Alabama things were a lot different and unequal between Blacks and Whites
He knew that Jim Crow laws and segregation were the way of life in the South
And he knew this was not the way the world was supposed to be

Jimmie Lee Jackson dreamed of a better life and believed in a new day
After being inspired by Dr. Martin Luther King, Jr. and others to stand up for change and to fight for their God-given rights and rights as American citizens
He made a commitment to help change how Blacks were being treated in the South
But little did he know that his bravery, courage and taking a stance against the only way of life he knew would cost him his life!
Little did he know that his death would lead to a historic protest march from Selma to Montgomery!
A march that came to be known as Bloody Sunday
And because of the media attention of the police brutality of that march combined with his martyrdom death
He helped to play a strong role in the passing of the Voting Rights Act of 1965!
Jimmie Lee Jackson would become one of the many people who would sacrifice and give their life for the rights of Black people and for social change in America
He was not looking to personally make history, but his name became entrenched in American history forever
Forty-five years, nine months and thirteen days
And for Jimmie Lee Jackson February 18, 1965 was the day he met his fate
Because on this day after meeting at the Zion United Methodist Church in Marion, Alabama
And participating in an attempted peaceful protest to free a jailed civil rights worker
Jimmie Lee Jackson and roughly five hundred other protestors were attacked by police
Not for committing a crime or breaking the law
But for protesting for justice and a better way of life
They were making a statement that enough was enough and that the second class citizenship way of life had to change
And that Black people had a right to vote in the state of Alabama

But the law was not on their side that day
Law enforcement on that day had come to defend a system of status quo
Law enforcement had become the criminal minded and attacked defenseless and unarmed men, women, and children
Attacking and beating the citizens they were sworn to protect and serve
And after being chased into a local café with his mother and eighty-two year old grandfather
And attempting to protect them from the beatings of Alabama state troopers
Jimmie Lee Jackson was critically shot, beaten, and lay in the street for two hours before he was taken to a hospital for treatment
Eight days later Jimmie Lee Jackson was dead
And for over forty years
Justice was un-served!
No charges!
No arrests!
No justice for all!
And no closure for the family of Jimmie Lee Jackson
The case had barely been investigated and was filed in the cold case cabinet for what seemed to be forever
The name of his killer was kept a public mystery until 2004 when James Fowler admitted to being the shooter
And it took another three years after Fowler's confession for him to be indicted and another three years to be convicted
James Fowler remained an Alabama state trooper and was never reprimanded for his actions
He was never even asked about the Jimmie Lee Jackson case by all those who supposedly investigated the case
But more than four decades after this fatal shooting
A painful chapter in U.S. history has been closed and this journey for justice is now complete
And we can close the book on one of the many Civil Rights era cold case murders

After forty-five years, nine months and thirteen days
The spirit of Jimmie Lee Jackson found a little justice and a little peace
James Fowler will now serve his time
And I guess we can say justice has been served
Or can we?
But one thing is for certain!
And that is Jimmie Lee Jackson helped to change America forever

Float like a Butterfly and Sting like a Bee

Float like a butterfly
Sting like a bee
There was no one greater than the man known as Muhammad Ali
A champion in the ring and an ambassador to the world
He said "I am the greatest"
And the greatest he was
Charismatic, entertaining and poetic was he
No one carried himself like Muhammad Ali
Born Cassius Marcellus Clay
The Louisville Slugger
He was born to be a champion
A champion like no other
Powerful, quick, and destroying all that came
It was almost like he was born to be king of the ring
Float like a butterfly
Sting like a bee
There was no one greater than the man known as Muhammad Ali
He was agile, fast and strong and hands could not hit what eyes could not see
There was no one in the same class as Muhammad Ali
He was confident, self promoting, and had a style of his own
With his Ali shuffle, Rope-a-dope, and lighting quick jabs
He would predict the round in which his opponents would fall
From "The Thrilla in Manila" to the "Rumble in the Jungle"
From Cooper, Quarry, Patterson, and Terrell
Ali fought them all
And all became victims of Ali's predictive round calls
Liston, Frazier, Norton, and Big George
Ali became legendary as he beat them all

But more importantly, he has always answered the humanitarian call
He has traveled the world
Helping people in need and touching many lives
From heavyweight boxing champion to friend of the world
Float like a butterfly
Sting like a bee
There was no one greater than the man known as Muhammad Ali
A champion in the ring and an ambassador to the world
He said "I am the greatest"
And the greatest he was

Malcolm and Martin

Brother Malcolm and Brother Martin
So different, yet they had so much in common
Their beliefs, ideologies, and philosophies were different
Their journey and paths were different
But because of their commitment to uplift their people
Their lives were quite similar
Malcolm and Martin
Martin and Malcolm
Men who believed that one day there would be a new America
An America where all people would be treated equally
An America that would not be a divided nation
An America where everyone could enjoy the rights guaranteed by the Constitution
An America where we could say we have overcome and there would be no need to pursue true democracy by any means necessary
Malcolm and Martin
Martin and Malcolm
They were summoned by their past to help change the future of their people
They heard the voices of their ancestors
They heard the shouts from the bottom of the slave ships during the journeys of the Middle Passage
They heard the cries of the slave mother as her child was pulled from her arms and sold to a new slave owner
They heard the whispers as runaway slaves communicated with each other while they followed the North Star to freedom
They heard the yells of people calling for help during the race riots
And they heard the songs of the spirituals sang during the long days working the fields

They were motivated and inspired to change America because of their people's history
Malcolm and Martin
Martin and Malcolm
They believed that all people were God's people
And that all people deserved to be treated with the same dignity, love, and respect
They believed that one day this nation would rise up and live out the true meaning of its creed
That all people are created equal
They believed that America needed to be transformed
And that a change would one day come
Malcolm and Martin
Martin and Malcolm
They were men with a dream and men that had a vision
A dream and vision that was more than personal
A dream and vision of a better America for them and their families
A dream and vision of a better America for not just black people, but for all people
A dream and vision for black people to have an equal opportunity to fulfill their dreams and to live out their lives to their full potential
Their dreams and vision became the pulse that strengthen and lifted up broken people
Malcolm and Martin
Martin and Malcolm
Men who were brave and held their heads up high
They were men who challenged their people and America with a message
A message for their people to have courage, to stand up and to be strong
A message of self-determination, motivation, and sacrifice
A message for black people to believe in themselves and to fight for their God-given rights

A message that did not show any fear in the speaking out against the wrongs in America
A message that demanded for America to change
A message that called for the human and civil rights for black people in America
And though their philosophies and journeys were different
Their goal was the same
And that was to transform America
Malcolm and Martin
Martin and Malcolm
Reluctant heroes
It was not their goal to become historical icons
It was not their goal to lead a race of people in their fight for liberty, justice, and equality
It was not their goal to give their lives at the age of thirty-nine for a better America
It was not their goal to leave their families without husbands and fathers
And that was the ultimate sacrifice they paid for a better tomorrow for those they loved
So heroes they were
Malcolm and Martin
Martin and Malcolm
They knew America's history and the realities for black people during their day
They knew the shame of a nation
And how deeply rooted prejudice, racism, and discrimination were in this land called America
They knew freedom and true democracy would not be free
They took an American problem and made it a world matter
Their courage, bravery, and thirst for change helped to change America forever
They navigated their people through the darkness of second class citizenship and into the brightness of a new day
Malcolm and Martin
Martin and Malcolm

They were cultural, political, and social revolutionaries
A Christian and a Muslim
A Southerner and a Northerner
College educated and street educated
I will turn my cheek and I will defend myself
So different, but so much in common
And though they only met once briefly
The perfect picture of them together maybe said what they were never able to say
Malcolm and Martin
Martin and Malcolm
Had a lot in common

Tommie Smith and John Carlos made One Great Stance

Tommie Smith and John Carlos made a statement on October 16, 1968
On an evening when a silent protest created a lasting image
A symbolic image that was so powerful that it painted a picture of America to the world
An image that told the story of America's not so beautiful past
And a story of America's turbulent present at that time
During the 1968 Olympics, Tommie Smith and John Carlos stood strong in protest
Their protest was not anti-American
But it was a protest calling for America to be what it was founded to be
It was a protest for equality and freedom for blacks in America
It was a protest to eliminate the injustices black Americans were facing everyday in America
Two-hundred meters in 19.83 seconds and Tommie Smith crossed the finish line setting a world record while Australian Peter Norman and John Carlos finished a Close second and third
Their Olympic success and protest created a picture that would forever be remembered
While the world was watching
The 1968 Olympics became the forum
And the world was the audience
The world of sports and politics collided when three champions went to the podium to accept their medals
Two Americans and an Australian painted a picture for the world to see
Tommie Smith receiving the gold medal
Peter Norman receiving the silver medal
John Carlos receiving the bronze medal

As they all stood in solidarity wearing the Olympic Project for Human Rights badge to protest the racism and exploitation of black Athletes in America
And as the "Star Spangled Banner" played they began their historic protest
With their heads bowed Tommie Smith and John Carlos raised their black gloved clenched fists
Tommie Smith with his right hand covered and John Carlos with his left hand covered stood with pride and courage
Their raised clenched fists representing Black power
They received their medals shoeless with black socks which represented the poverty of blacks in America
Tommie Smith wore a black scarf around his neck representing Black pride
John Carlos wore beads that represented those who have died because of American racism
A box carried by Tommie Smith held a small olive branch that represented peace
Their protest set the stage for other protests during the Olympics
But these other protestors didn't paint the picture to the world of the plight of black people in America that Tommie Smith and John Carlos presented
The protest that became front page news around the world was a heavy price to pay for Tommie Smith and John Carlos
They were immediately expelled from the US Olympic team and their medals were confiscated
They and their families received death threats and they were ostracized by America
They became cursed heroes
But Tommie Smith and John Carlos were heroes and they helped to change America
America needs to thank them for the price they were willing to pay for change in America

Sometimes America Needs to Remember the Orangeburg Massacre

Sometimes we do not remember the price that was paid for change
Sometimes we forget the stories and graphic images of an America that did not resemble the America we observe today
Sometimes we forget the changing of America did not happen without a heavy cost
Sometimes we forget how many people paid the ultimate price for a change in America
In 1968, we witnessed the assassinations of Dr. Martin Luther King and Robert Kennedy
In 1968, we witnessed the Olympic protests of Tommie Smith and John Carlos
In 1968, we witnessed the passing and signing of a Civil Rights Act
But in 1968 we also witnessed the Orangeburg Massacre
February 8, 1968 is a day that is seldom spoken about or remembered
A day Samuel Hammond, Delano Middleton, and Henry Smith paid that ultimate price for change
A day when about 200 college students gathered on the campus of South Carolina State University to protest the segregation of a local bowling alley
A day when a peaceful demonstration turned into one of the saddest days in America's history
February 8, 1968 is a day that America should never forget
Because on this day after tensions began to rise, the local police in Orangeburg, South Carolina opened fire
Killing three students and injuring twenty-seven others
During a peaceful protest designed to make a statement that segregation needed to end
And that enough was enough
Instead ended in bloodshed, violence, and tragedy

Instead ended in three young men never afforded the opportunities to fulfill their dreams
Instead turned into a day that received very little media coverage nationally and was hidden in America's past
This seldom mentioned incident of America's past also paints a picture of the injustice of America's past
Because even though there was an investigation and nine officers were brought to trial on charges of excessive force against a group of unarmed student protestors on a college campus
All nine officers were acquitted of all charges
In fact, the only person who was charged and sent to prison was Cleveland Sellers
A student who was convicted and later pardoned for inciting the riot that led to the shootings
Sometimes bringing to light the memory of a forgotten and ignored incident in America's past
Reminds America of its journey as a nation
And forces the examination of the scarred justice of America and what it has taken for America to be where it is today
It reminds America of the importance of connecting America's past to the present and future of America
It reminds America the price that was paid for change was not in vain
And that the lives and actions of college students on February 8, 1968 was not in vain
Sometimes America needs to remember

Martin Luther King, Jr. Had a Dream

Martin Luther King, Jr. had a dream
He believed in the American dream
He believed that one day this nation
Would rise up and live out the true meaning of its American creed
He believed that all men were created equal
Martin Luther King Jr. had a dream
He believed in the future of America
He believed in the future of his people
His dream was not for Blacks to stop striving for the dream
Martin Luther King, Jr. had a dream
His dream was not for Blacks to continue to suffer from
Discrimination, hate, and racism
His dream was not for Blacks to continue to struggle from
Depression and oppression
His dream was not for Blacks to be left behind
In a world that was moving forward
Martin Luther King, Jr. had a dream
He dreamed that we as a people could
Live together
Pray together
Work together
And make this world a better place together
He never dreamed of broken family structures
Women playing the roles of both mother and father
And grandparents raising their grandchildren
He never dreamed of Black men filling the prison systems
Or the high rates of Blacks in unemployment, high school dropouts, and teenage pregnancy
Martin Luther King, Jr. had a dream
He dreamed that one day his four little children
Would one day live in a nation where they would not be judged by the color of their skin, but by the content of their character!

He never dreamed we would no longer care about our character or integrity
Or about whom we are and what we are
He never dreamed that some people would forget about the struggles of our past and about the price that was paid so that we could be all that we could be
He never dreamed that the giving of his life
Or the lost lives of many others was given in vain
Martin Luther King, Jr. had a dream
And that dream was not for us to be
Enslaved again! Enslaved again! My God Almighty, why are we enslaved again!
He never dreamed for us to become mental slaves to emancipation and gains
He never dreamed for us to be shackled by the success and progress of our people
Martin Luther King, Jr. had a dream

Arthur Ashe

Arthur Ashe knew who he was
And he knew his calling and purpose
He was a pioneer
And he defined greatness in the sport of tennis
During a time when the road he traveled he had to travel alone
His legacy does not receive the respect it deserves
Because now could not be possible
If it was not for Arthur Ashe and many others then
He was committed to his calling and purpose
He was committed to his journey
Being a prisoner to what he was born to be
He responded and showed the world that he was a champion
He was extraordinary, great, and spectacular
And played the game of tennis with a passion and a quiet intensity that had never been seen
Words simply could not describe Arthur Ashe
Failing was not an option
He played the game as if he was the only one on the court
His heart, dedication, desire, and focus defined his greatness as an athlete and as a man
He endured much resistance and many obstacles
Fighting racism and discrimination
And against incredible odds
He became one of the most dynamic athletes in the history of sports
Arthur Ashe made a difference
His legacy was more than a great tennis player
His legacy was who he was as a man
He was a humble man of principle and purpose
He stood strongly for what was right and for what he believed
And he was not silent about issues in the world during his life
He spoke out against racism, discrimination, apartheid, and the plight of the Haitian refugees

Up until his death, he used his personal battle with AIDS as a platform to raise awareness of AIDS and for a cure for the deadly disease that would take his own life
He was an activist who fought for all people
He was a man who made a difference
He was more than a Black man
He was a great man who left an enormous legacy and a lasting impression on the world
And helped to make the world a better place
He was a man who forced change
A change in sports and in society
Arthur Ashe knew who he was
A man who was committed to his calling and purpose
A man who was committed to his journey
Arthur Ashe was a great man who helped to change the world

I Accept Your Apology, America

I accept your apology
Though it is over 140 years late
But an apology for slavery was long over due
And I will start by accepting whatever America is willing to give
But America does not think this is a compromise
And that this apology is enough
I still feel and still want America to finish apologizing
And I do not want America to think that all of the apologizing should be complete
No America!
A simple resolution from a few states for their past acts is not enough
A resolution should not be enough for over two hundred years of slavery and for the acts of abuse, discrimination, and disrespect for almost another 150 years after slavery
A resolution should not be enough for committing one of the greatest crimes and human injustices ever
A resolution and some late apologies is the best you can do, America?
America how can you apologize for slavery
The institution that has been dead legally for over 140 years
But not apologize for the legacy of slavery
And the effects of slavery on Black people since it ended
So America I use your apology as a platform to ask for more apologies
America, apologize for the evils that slavery created
Apologize for how slavery destroyed families and culture
Apologize for the long term mental and psychological effects of slavery
Apologize for the period of America's history black people were legally labeled as less than a human being
You see America, the apologizing should not stop with a simple apology and resolution

By accepting this long overdue apology America, allow it to be the beginning of acknowledging many of the wrongs of the past and making amends
So let us start apologizing, America
And let us start with failing to acknowledge Black history and failing to tell an accurate and complete story of American history in our history books
America, apologize for not treating Black people with dignity and respect
America, apologize for the post-slavery injustices towards Black people up until today
Apologize for racial, educational, and job discrimination
Apologize for the Jim Crow laws and institutional racism
Apologize for the murders, lynching, and actions of hate towards Blacks in America
Apologize for a history of not defending a defenseless people
Apologize for needing affirmative action laws and civil rights legislation to ensure equality and justice and to protect the rights of Black people
Apologize for the government's covert attacks and undeclared war against Black leaders
Apologize for the race riots in Tulsa, Wilmington, and other cities
And once you start apologizing
Do not forget to apologize for failing to follow through with the promised, "forty acres and a mule"
I will accept your apology America
But I will also ask that you study your past America
And hopefully you will understand there is a lot more to apologize for
And for now I will say thank you and accept these apologies

We Have Forgotten So Much

It is amazing
How we have come so far
And accomplished so much
And all of this in such a short period of time
But it is also tragic
How we have forgotten so much
In such a short period of time
We seem to have forgotten
The price that was paid
So that we can do what we do
And live where we live
And work where we work
We have forgotten
The fight and struggles for our human and civil rights
We have forgotten our journey
It was not so long ago everything was separate and not at all equal
Racism was strong and Black people had to deal with blatant discrimination daily
It was not so long ago
We had Black and white restrooms and water fountains
And Blacks had to ride on the back of buses
And enter stores and restaurants from the rear
It was not that long ago
We had inferior education, housing, and health care
It is deep how we have forgotten
How we had marched, protested, sat-in, and fought for equality
And how we no longer remember those that paved the way for us to be where we are today
And how we no longer remember the price that was paid during our great journey
It is sad when you ask many Black people about the journey of Black people and they cannot tell you of the contributions and sacrifices of their own people

And of the many people who dedicated and sacrificed their lives during the fight for equality
It is heartbreaking when black children know very little about their ancestors and about their people's journey
Who committed themselves so these black children could be all they could be
We have truly lost scope of where we have come from and how far we have traveled
The unity and pride that we once had has been replaced by an "it is all about me" mentality
The voice for change, equality, and progress is gone
The commitment to be conscious and to be viewed positively has disappeared
And has been replaced by negative images and stereotypes encouraged by the media and a world out to exploit who we are for the mighty dollar
And sadly, even the exploitation has been supported and glorified by Black people
The state of Black America has become a story of a people suffering from selective amnesia
And it is deep how we have forgotten so much in such a short period of time

I Am an American

I am an American
I am not a Democrat or Republican
I am not a conservative or liberal
Because I do not think any of these groups have defined me, nor have they truly accepted me
But I am an American
I am not always embraced by America
Or treated like an American
But I am an American
A descendant of victims of America's past
A past that America is not proud to talk about
But a past that is a part of America's history
A past that welcomes you to my world
A past that molded and motivated me
A past that developed and made me who I am
An African-American
But I am still an American
I am an American
And America is me
Even though America has not always embraced me
I have never stopped dreaming my American dream and of what America could be
But I am an American
And even though the journey has been long
And the battles have been many
And even though I must dot my "I's"
And cross my "T's"
And work twice as hard
To receive my due
I am an American
And even though I am still viewed
By the color of my skin
And I still fall victim at times to the same discrimination, prejudice, and racism that my ancestors faced

*I still view myself as an American
I was born in America
I was raised in America
And I will die in America
My ancestors' sweat and blood helped to build America
A price was paid for equality and freedom
A price was paid to have an equal education and for the right to vote
And because of the price that was paid to be an American and because of a journey that has gone from chains to the White House
I will always call myself an American*

A Defining Day (Barack Obama)

November 4, 2008 has become a defining day in America's history
Because on that day
The reality is America made a statement that it was ready for change
And it decided the time is now
Because after eight years
America needed a light of hope
And Barack Obama has become that great beacon of light
Barack Obama has given America a change it can believe in
A change that is deeply rooted in the American dream
A change that transcends race, color, creed, or political affiliation
A change that was for everyone
As true democracy was awakened
And as we witnessed history being accomplished
A picture of a new and better tomorrow was painted for the world to see
A picture that was the fulfillment of what America was built as and promised
A picture that was deeper than the political philosophies of the Democrats or Republicans
Barack Obama offered America a new hope
As the 44th President of the United States
He inherited a nation that has defined democracy
But he also inherited a nation that has a past
Because many Americans thought they would never see such a day in their lifetime
The day that America did not judge by the color of one's skin, but by the content of one's character
On that glorious day

America could say during this defining moment in American history
That the reality is no longer that a black man could never be president
But the reality is America elected a black President
Nearly five decades after the greatest demonstration for freedom in America's history
Nearly five decades after the signing of the Voting Rights Act of 1965
On November 4, 2008, freedom rings in America
And even though the images of America's past still resonate before us
America's future is bright
Because Barack Obama transcends race
Barack Obama is a strong leader
Who is competent, passionate, and committed to America!
He is for what America is supposed to stand for
What Barack Obama means to America
Is that America is for all Americans
And their inalienable rights of life, liberty and the pursuit of happiness can be fulfilled
The American dream
Barack Obama's journey is the picture of what it means to be an American
Barack Obama is for making America a nation we can all believe in
Barack Obama is for making America a nation we can be proud of now and tomorrow
Yes! November 4, 2008 was a defining day in America's history

Barack Obama

Who would have thought that America, with a history so great
Yet with a historical legacy of a divided nation
Would elect Barack Obama as the 44th President of the United States?
Nearly two hundred and fifty years of slavery and forced labor
People being sold and branded as property
And labeled as less than a human being
But today we have President Barack Obama
America! With all of its glory
And still a nation damaged from its past
But who would have thought?
After the ending of slavery in America nearly one hundred and fifty years ago
America still gave birth to Jim Crow and to another one hundred years that America is not proud to share or put in its history books
America has failed to tell the stories of Wilmington, North Carolina; Springfield, Illinois; and Tulsa Oklahoma and how African-Americans' democracy was taken from them
But today America has a President named Barack Obama
America! With a history that needed acts and amendments to legally give everyone civil and human rights
Those same acts and amendments still failed to guarantee the right to vote for all
America the land of the free
America! With a history that included a cast of characters that are not always remembered or mentioned when America's story is being recounted
Because America does not always tell you about Emmitt Till, James Chaney, or the victims of the Tuskegee Syphilis Study
Or about four little girls named Denise McNair, Cynthia Wesley, Carole Robertson and Addie Mae Collins who lost their lives after their church was bombed in Birmingham, Alabama

America does not like telling all of its history and of its journey as a nation
But today a new era dawns in America
Two hundred and twenty years after America named its first president
A slave-owning president named George Washington
President Barack Obama has become the symbol of the red, white, and blue
A symbol of equality, hope, and true democracy
Because even after boycotts, protests, and sit-ins
And after the freedom rides and a Bloody Sunday
And after a March on Washington and the killing of a King
America has taken a step towards becoming a more perfect union
And as America embraces Barack Obama as its 44th President
America must also examine its past to understand America's present and America's future
Because this is a historic achievement that many in America thought could never happen and would never happen
But today America!
We have a new day and a new era

The Inheritance

The right to vote should be viewed as an inheritance
Something very valuable passed down from our ancestors
The ancestors who fought, sacrificed, and died to give a gift
A priceless gift
But the inheritance is also the story of the journey to obtain the gift
An inheritance that has become a symbol of the equality obtained during that journey
An inheritance that has become a symbol of the freedom obtained during that journey
An inheritance that has become a symbol of the justice and liberty obtained during that journey
An inheritance that defines democracy and a gift that defines America
Because the right for all Americans to vote is true democracy
America is a nation headed by leaders who are elected by the people to serve the people
The right to vote is the right to have a voice in America
A voice to be heard and recognized
One of the most precious gifts we have in America is the right to vote
A gift with a history that reveals the challenges, resistance, and struggles that were faced in an effort to prevent the inheritance
A gift that has always dealt with opposition in its effort to exist
So has America ever truly respected the inheritance and does true democracy exist?
Because once again the right to vote in America is under attack
As a movement that wants to take away the right to vote sits around hallucinating about a return to the good old days of a divided nation
Many in America struggle to determine if these attacks are reality or just an illusion

While others go back and forth between selective amnesia and immoral amnesia and choosing to ignore this all-out attack on one of the basic rights supposedly guaranteed by America
The facts are America is being attacked and we are not doing much to protect America against these attacks!
During these troubling times those who truly care about America must fight and protect the right to vote in America
Because in order to truly be a democracy there must be democracy for all people
To some in America, democracy has run its course
The right to vote that we have come to take for granted
May be lost for many voters who were once eligible
This war that has been declared within our nation
Means that the fundamental right to vote is threatened
America is 236 years old, and for 236 years America has been struggling with democracy
Either suppressing or attempting to suppress the right to vote for many Americans
Voter suppression and disfranchisement are nothing new in America
Neither is the fight for the right to vote in America
We must resist the attempts to establish new voting laws
That are reminiscent of some of the restrictive laws of the Jim Crow era
We must end the silence and bring an end to these attempts to make it harder to cast a vote
We must say no to the new voter identification requirements
That are becoming laws in some states
We must not forget the past as we deal with the present
So as we watch the latest episode of politicians gone wild
It does not matter if it is a presidential, congressional, state, or local election
The right to vote must be protected and ensured in America
Because one vote represents one voice
The Voting Rights Act of 1965 was passed to protect the rights of minority voters

So we must fight hard to protect our inheritance
The fact is there was a price that was paid for the right to vote
And we must never forget the challenges, experiences, and struggles
Of the journey that gave us this inheritance
The protected right to vote for all Americans is a gift that must be treasured
We must never take for granted the right to vote
We must never believe that the right to vote does not matter
We must speak out against any attacks on the right to vote
And we must raise awareness about protecting the right to vote
We must protect the right of every American citizen
To have an equal opportunity and right to vote
The right to vote is what is beautiful about America
Voting is a part of what defines democracy in America
It is the right to vote that makes America the nation that it is
The right to vote should be the voice of equality, freedom, and justice in America
The right to vote should help define the American dream
The right to vote should be as American as apple pie
The right to vote is worth fighting to protect
The right to vote is the gift that should always be passed down and treasured
And we as Americans should never allow anyone or anything to steal that right away
We must never forget the importance and the value of the right to vote
We must never forget the significance and value of our inheritance
We have an obligation to vote and to protect the right to vote
Because this is our inheritance

Today Barack Obama is President

Many people thought they would never see the day
The United States of America would have a Black President
But today Barack Obama is President
Elected by the many races of people that make up America
All shades of God's people making a choice
A choice to go against America's past
A choice that shows America's future
Many people died dreaming
Dreaming of a day that America would be a nation of true democracy
Dreaming of a day that America practiced what it preached to the world
And in the Constitution, Declaration of Independence, and the Bill of Rights
Many people thought they would never see the day
When they truly believed they were the "We the People" in order to form a more perfect Union as described in the Constitution
A day when they could say America was for all Americans
Regardless of race, color, or creed
A day when America's past reconciled with America's present
And gave hope to America's future
Many people thought they would never see the day
They could have change they could believe in
Or they would be a member of the generation that would no longer have to live convincing themselves that Martin Luther King's speech would one day come true
Because today "I Have a Dream" has become reality
Many people never thought they would see the day
They would no longer sing "We Shall Overcome"
And they could now say we have overcome
And the journey from 1619 to today
Would take them from slavery to Head of State
Many people never thought they would see the day

*When they could proudly say the price that was paid for equality
And the sacrifices for freedom
Were worth the ultimate reward
And the many people who marched, protested, and sacrificed their lives
For the American dream
Did not do so in vain
Many people thought they would never see the day
When they could say they have experienced what America stood for
Freedom, justice, and liberty
And witnessed the fulfillment of the American dream for all Americans
Because what used to be a dream is now a reality!
Many people thought they would never see the day
But it is a new day
And today Barack Obama is President*

Let Us Not Forget to Vote!

Let us not forget!
African-Americans did not always have the right to vote
Not far removed from a past that reveals their exclusion from the promises of America
The promises ensured by the Constitution
The promise that all are created equal
The promise of freedom, liberty, and justice
The promise of an electoral democracy
The promise of universal suffrage
These promises that defined America
But these truths that were supposed to be self-evident
Were not so true for African-Americans
Because for African-Americans, a price had to be paid for the right to vote
Because for African-Americans, the right to vote was not free
From the chains of slavery and being called three-fifths of a human being
To "Free at last! Free at last! Thank God Almighty we're free at last!"
From Thomas Mundy Peterson being the first African-American to cast a vote after the passing of the 15th Amendment
To Bloody Sunday and being attacked and beaten on the Edmund Pettus Bridge
From Andrew Goodman, Herbert Lee, James Chaney, Jimmie Lee Jackson, Medgar Evers, and Michael Schwerner dying for the right to vote
To Bob Moses and Mississippi Freedom Summer
And Fannie Lou Hamer "Being sick and tired of being sick and tired" and asking "Is this America?"
And let us not forget the martyrdom of a King
From a Civil War to a Civil Rights Movement
From the 13th, 14th, and 15th Amendments to the Constitution that were supposed to give African-Americans equality and the right to vote

To the need for Civil Rights and Voting Right Acts to ensure and protect those rights
Let us not forget we have a debt to pay to those that paved the way
The sacrifices that were made so all people could vote
We must not forget
Let us not forget that African-Americans did not always have the right to vote
Facing constant obstacles, opposition, and resistance and having to defy great odds
African-Americans had to fight for this precious right
They had to fight against literacy tests, poll taxes, grandfather clauses and gerrymandering
They were threatened by the terrorist acts of those who resisted the centuries old battle for change
The message for "Change we can believe in" was not a new message
African-Americans marched and protested for the freedom that was supposed to come with being an American
They fought for liberty
They fought for equality
They fought for justice
And many people paid the ultimate price and died for this precious gift given to us by those martyrs
So let us not be silent and let us exercise our hard fought right to vote
Because the journey is not complete and the work is not done
We were once disfranchised and we must not disfranchise ourselves
Voting is a privilege that was hard to come by
And indecision is a decision to not practice the fundamental right of true democracy
Not voting is not honoring and remembering those who fought the battle for voting rights and representation
We have an obligation and responsibility to cast our votes
We have to recapture the enthusiasm that fulfilled a dream

The dream that we can believe in change
The nation cheered and praised the slogan "Change we can believe in"
But America's problems are not a quick fix and change does not occur overnight
Change requires commitment and change requires time
We have gone from the slave ships to the White House and we cannot afford to stop there
We have to keep moving forward and towards brighter days
Every single vote has value and it is a voice
A vote to protect legislative and legal milestones
A vote to protect the achievements of the Civil Rights Movement
A vote to be included in the political process of America
A vote to continue this journey towards freedom, equality, and justice for all
A vote that says we're not going back and that we're only going forward
A vote to say thank you and to pay a debt to those that made voting a cherished right and a sacred duty
As our future lies before us
Let us not be silent and let us march to the ballot boxes
Because voting is more than a right for African-Americans
It is a responsibility
Let us not forget!
Let us vote!

January 15th

Every January 15th
We celebrate the life of Dr. Martin Luther King, Jr.
We celebrate how from 1955 to 1968
For only 13 years
Dr. King committed his life to fighting against the ills of America
He fought for the rights of Black people
Their God-given rights
He boycotted, marched, protested, and led a movement
So that everyone
Regardless of race, color, or creed
Would be able to live the American dream
Dr. King gave his life for his dream
And every January 15th we celebrates his legacy
But a King was not the only one to die
Many people fought just as hard
And some even paid the ultimate price of life
Just like Dr. King
But we only celebrate one day for a King
Though this day is well-deserved
Let us not forget the price that others paid
Let us not forget Medgar Evers
Who fought for the civil rights of Black people in Mississippi
And was gunned down in front of his home?
Let us not forget Rosa Parks
Who because of her refusal to give up her seat on a bus
Initiated the beginning of the civil rights movement
Let us not forget James Chaney
Who was murdered while registering blacks to vote in Mississippi?
Let us not forget the "Little Rock Nine"

Nine black students who were blocked from entering their school by the Governor of Arkansas and despite a year of violent threats manage to graduate
Let us not forget the four black students in Greensboro, NC who began a sit-in at a segregated lunch counter
Let us not forget the marches and protests
And the many people that fought in the army of a movement for freedom and justice
Let us not forget the victims of hate crimes and lynchings
Let us not forget on January 15th
To not only remember a King on his birthday
A holiday that was fought so hard to have
But let us take a moment to remember everyone that fought and sacrificed for justice
Let us remember all of those who will never have a holiday

A Day to Remember (The Brown Decision Under Attack)

A day to remember
June 28, 2007 is a day we must never forget
A day the Supreme Court has returned America to its not so glorious days of the past
Of segregation and separate, but not necessarily equal
From Plessy versus Ferguson
To Brown versus Board of Education
And back again
The Supreme Court decision
Placing limitations on the use of race in assigning students to public schools
Has damaged the legacy of the Brown versus Board of Education ruling
It has damaged the legacy of the efforts and gains of the Supreme Court in 1954
Led by then Chief Justice Earl Warren
It has damaged the legacy of the brave acts of the Little Rock Nine and Ruby Bridges
It has damaged the legacy of the Civil Rights Movement
And it has damaged the legacy of everything it has taken to get America to where it is today
We must ask was all of this in vain?
As Charles Hamilton Houston and Thurgood Marshall turn in their graves
The Supreme Court where they strongly presented the landmark case
Has reversed the gains that have been protected by law
America has taken a step backwards
Returning to a time that we truly do not want to remember
A time when everything in society was influenced by prejudice, racism, and discrimination
A time when everything was separate and unequal

The 1954 decision declared the system of legal segregation unconstitutional
But our great court has decided to change the laws that were designed to ensure equality and to protect the rights of all people
Race should not matter, but it still does
And legal support for re-segregation is not the answer
Even though America had never killed segregation
Segregation has been able to survive and segregationists have been able to regroup and gain this victory
School desegregation is no longer a Black/White paradigm
All minorities are affected by this decision
History is being unmade
And a 5 to 4 court decision has set the precedent for future decisions
A decision that could affect affirmative action, college admissions, employment, hiring, and government contracting
We are living in a nation where minorities will soon form the majority
And if we are going to succeed in living together
Then we need diversity and integration
And not segregation
So the day the Brown versus Board of Education decision of 1954 was attacked is a day we must always remember

Freedom Was Not Free

As we open the book of America's past
And decipher through the history of America
We will discover that freedom did not come the same way for all Americans
We will discover that the journey for freedom was different for African-Americans
Because when Thomas Jefferson wrote that "All men are created equal"
Those words did not embrace and include the African-Americans as citizens of this nation, but as property of this nation
And the principles of liberty, justice, and equality took some time to include all Americans
The connection of the past to the present
And remembering almost 400 hundred years of a legacy of slavery, racism, and discrimination will remind us that freedom was not free for African-Americans
Their gateway to America and its American dream did not come through the gates of Ellis Island
Their gateway was the slave docks that welcomed them to America
And there was no need for dreams, because dreams very seldom came true if you were not free
But if you follow the trail for freedom for African-Americans you will find their trail of tears
Because in order to be free you had to be freed from something
And the horrors of slavery, segregation, Jim Crow laws, disfranchisement, lynching and race riots brought many tears
And the freedom for African-Americans was not free
The price for freedom was the scars of slavery and post reconstruction
The price for freedom has been the psychological damage of "Separate but Equal"
The price for freedom was the murders of Emmitt Till and Medgar Evers

The price for freedom were the marches of Birmingham, Montgomery and Selma
The price for freedom was the protests of the Freedom Riders and the sit-ins at lunch counters
The price for freedom was the court battles of the NAACP and the fight for equality
Freedom was not free
Letters from a Birmingham jail and the Children's Crusades
Should be a reminder that freedom was not free
A March on Washington and "I Have a Dream"
Should be a reminder that freedom was not free
The images of people being beaten by police, bitten by dogs, and blasted by fire hoses
Should be a reminder that freedom was not free
The images of James Meredith entering the University of Mississippi with federal troops by his side should be a reminder that freedom was not free
The registering of voters in the South and the crusades of CORE, SNCC and SCLC should be a reminder that freedom was not free
As we examine and study this open book of America's past
And how African-Americans have gone from chains to change to the White House
The reality of the African-American experience
Is that freedom was not free

What Is American History?

What is American history?
Incomplete if it does not accurately include the history of African-American people
From America's beginning until now
The African-American presence in American history cannot be denied
A lot of it is great, but unfortunately much of it is very painful
The African-American's place in American history cannot be denied
But sadly, America has done a remarkable job of hiding much of its own history
By only telling the history that makes America resemble a great democracy and nation
Concealing the truths that damages the world's image of America
But America cannot boast about the good of its past without acknowledging the not so good
Yes! America has a great history, but it is time to come correct about its past
The past the history books do not want to acknowledge or go into great detail about
Because even after there was freedom for America, there was still slavery in America
American slavery and the harsh and inhumane treatment of slaves is American history
How slaves helped to build America by forced labor and sweat is American history
And how many of America's founding fathers were slave owners is American history
But America only shares pieces of its history
The truth about Abraham Lincoln and the Emancipation Proclamation
And how this great American president and his proclamation really did not free the slaves is American history

American history is Jim Crow laws and the disfranchisement of millions of African-Americans
American history is lynching, race riots, segregation, and white only signs
And let us not forget about the FBI's Counter Intelligence Program and how America's abuse of human rights led to a Civil Rights Movement
The fight and struggles for freedom is American history
Unfortunately, this is also America's legacy
But African-Americans have also contributed greatly to America's history
African-Americans have strong contributions in the arts, education, medicine and science
And this is also American history
The contributions of Phyllis Wheatley, Langston Hughes, James Weldon Johnson and Paul Robeson are a part of American history
The contributions of Dr. Charles Drew, Dr. Ernest Just, Dr. Daniel Hale Williams, and Dr. Ben Carson are a part of American history
The contributions of Lewis Latimer, Elijah McCoy, and Garrett Morgan are a part of American history
And educators like Horace Mann Bond, George Washington Carver, John Hope Franklin, Benjamin Mays, and Melvin Tolson are a part of American history
American history is Crispus Attucks, Gabriel Prosser, Denmark Vesey, and Nat Turner
American history is Sojourner Truth, Dread Scott, Marcus Garvey, and Ida B. Wells
American history is W.E.B Du Bois, A. Phillip Randolph, Mary McLeod Bethune, Stokely Carmichael, the Black Panther Party, and the contributions and stories of many others
American history should be the whole story
And not just select portions or distortions of the past
Because the history of African-Americans is a part of the whole story of American history

And that is American history!

A Look in a Mirror

When looking in a mirror
You should see more than just a reflection of you
You should see a reflection of who you are
And a reflection of the journey it took for you to become who you are
A look in a mirror should reveal more than the external and the physical you
A look in a mirror should also reveal the internal and intimate makeup of who you are
Because the physical act of looking into a mirror is to see and examine one's self
A look in a mirror should reveal the resemblance of the parents that God had chosen for you
A look in a mirror should reveal the faces of those who were your primary caretakers
The faces of those who loved you more than words could truly tell
The faces of those who were family regardless of whether they were blood related or not
A look in a mirror would reveal the faces of those parents who took their God-given assignment seriously
A look in a mirror would reveal those grandparents, aunts, uncles, and other family members
Those who often have stepped up and accepted the role and responsibility of being caretakers and guardians that weren't initially theirs
A look in a mirror would reveal the faces of those who provided the daily prayers and life lessons that often carried and protected those whom they loved dearly
A look in a mirror would reveal the faces of those people in the community who gave those encouraging words freely

A look in a mirror would reveal the minds that would often come up with creative ideas and ways to say how much you were loved
A look in a mirror would reveal the hearts that were the life source for all of the love shown to you
A look in a mirror would reveal the protective arms that were wrapped around you when you were scared
A look in a mirror would reveal the hands that cared for you when you were sick
A look in a mirror would reveal the legs and feet that would walk you to and from school each day as a small child
A look in a mirror should be more than just a look in the mirror
A look in a mirror is the face of the father who worked two jobs to ensure all of your needs were met
A look in a mirror is the face of the mother who did not always have the money, but she always found a way to do what needed to be done
A look in a mirror is the faces of those committed people who put your needs first
The people in your life that loved you enough to make sure you ate well, dressed well and had your homework done
And who did their best to protect you from all that was negative in this world
A look in a mirror would reveal those special teachers who took a special interest in you
A look in a mirror reveals a journey
A look in a mirror reveals the two worlds that existed
A world united and a world divided
A world of dreams and a world of dreams deferred
A look in a mirror reveals the faces of the voices of the past whose words we can still hear advocating for generation after generation
A look in a mirror reveals the pioneers of the struggle for change in America
A look in a mirror reveals the faces of those fighters for equality, freedom, and justice

A look in a mirror reveals the faces of the unsung heroes whose names are seldom mentioned, but whose acts were great and heroic
A look in a mirror reveals the many faces of those who died and sacrificed their lives for you
The faces of those who never had the opportunity for a better opportunity or a chance to live the American dream
When you really examine yourself in a mirror it will reveal a lot more than the reflection you would see
A look in a mirror will reveal your past, present, and future
A look in a mirror will tell a story
A look in a mirror will reveal who you truly are

One Month

One month
I don't think so
To recognize
Realize
And be reminded that Black people have a history
One month
To remember the contributions
One month
To remember the struggles
One month
To remember the fight
One month
To remember the journey
Of a group of people that helped to build America
The fact is Black people in America have a history
Be it good or be it bad
Black people in America have a history
From slavery to now
America cannot deny Black History
America must remember Black history every month
And not just in February
But from January to December
Black history is every month
And Black history is American history

Four More Years

America has spoken
And again, it is President Barack Obama that has been chosen to lead America
Four more years confirm that America believed and continues to believe in President Barack Obama
Four more years confirm that the majority of America believes that Obama-cares about America
Four more years confirm that America is optimistic about its future
The heart of America believes in the leadership of President Barack Obama
The heart of America believes that America's best days are yet to come
America has spoken and President Barack Obama has been chosen to lead America for four more years
President Barack Obama, the 44th President of the United States, has been justified by the blueprints of American democracy
The vote count does not lie, because America has made its choice again
And America's choice again is President Barack Obama
Four years ago President Barack Obama gave us change that we could believe in
Four years ago President Barack Obama gave us the hope of a better future
Four years ago President Barack Obama gave America a vision that was for all Americans and not just for some Americans
Four years ago President Barack Obama started a journey to change America
Four years ago President Barack Obama gave everyone in America the ability to believe in the American dream
Four years ago was the beginning of a symbolic journey that helped America believe in four more years

The first four years were not easy, but President Barack Obama endured against attacks, challenges, and resistance from his opposition
He provided guidance and strong leadership during some tough times in America
When President Barack Obama was elected, America was faced with the worst financial crisis since the Great Depression
The American auto industry was on the verge of collapse
Over 30,000 Americans lived without health insurance
America was fighting two wars
In four years President Barack Obama's leadership helped America avoid a potentially catastrophic economic and financial meltdown
His leadership made universal healthcare the law of the land
As commander-in-chief, his war on terrorism proved steady and strong
Osama Bin Laden is no longer a threat to America
As commander-in-chief, he has worked hard to end the wars and to bring our troops home
If America is honest, it cannot deny President Barack Obama's achievements and his imprint on America and its future
President Barack Obama's first four years presented a strong case for four more years
And this great victory reveals that America believes in the president of the United States
Four more years of protecting the voices that have often been shut out of American democracy
Four more years of keeping the eye on the prize for a better America
America has spoken
And America desires President Barack Obama to take a second oath as president of the United States of America
And despite a major campaign to make the president a one term president
America believed that President Barack Obama was again the best choice to guide America into the future

America has made its choice again
And again it is President Barack Obama
President Barack Obama has been reelected for four more years

I Am My Blackness

I am my Blackness
I am the variety of the many complexions of the skin that defines me
I am the one drop of blood that is all that is needed to make me who I am
I am the glow of my light skin and the purity of my dark skin
I am my Blackness
I am my journey
I am the cargo of the slave ships
I am the runaway slave following the North Star to freedom
I am the callous and swollen hands that helped to build America
I am the soldier that fought and died for America in all of its wars
I am the protestor and freedom fighter who fought for the rights of all Americans
I am the legacy of my journey
I am my journey
I am my Blackness
I am my history
I am real history and not forgotten history
I am a contributor to what has made America a great nation
I am more than just twenty-eight days and I am worth more than forty acres and a mule
I am a creator, designer, educator, inventor and innovator
I am the dreams of Martin Luther King, Jr.
I am the courage of Malcolm X
I am the bravery of Rosa Parks
I am the strength of Jackie Robinson
I am the inspiration of Carter G. Woodson
I am the racial pride of Marcus Garvey
I am the perseverance of President Barack Obama
I am my history
I am my Blackness

I am the determination of Thurgood Marshall
I am the vision of W. E. B. DuBois
I am the rebellion of Nat Turner
I am the genius of Benjamin Banneker
I am the gifted hands of Dr. Ben Carson
I am the lost and unfulfilled life of Emmitt Till
I am my history
I am my Blackness
I am the words of Langston Hughes
I am the poetry of Phyllis Wheatley
I am the stories of Zora Neale Hurston
I am the paintings of Ernie Barnes
I am the music of Duke Ellington
I am the pictures of Gordon Parks
I am my history
I am my Blackness
I am the Buffalo Soldier
I am the Black Panther Party
I am the Harlem Renaissance
I am the spirit of the Civil Rights Movement
I am my incarcerated brother or sister
I am the gospel, jazz, rhythm and blues of my people
I am the struggle for equality, freedom and justice
I am my history
I am my Blackness
I am a victim of slavery
I am a victim of the mental, physical, and psychological damage that has endured since post slavery
I am a victim of Jim Crow
I am a victim of injustice towards Black people in America
I am a victim of Hurricane Katrina
I am a victim of the greatest Holocaust ever
I am a victim of the plight of my past
I am my history
I am my Blackness
I am a survivor

I am a survivor of my traumatic past
I am a survivor of the abuses of slavery
I am a survivor of the race riots throughout America
I am a survivor of being treated as a second class citizen and less than a human being
I am a survivor of "white only", separate but equal and not being able to vote
And I am also a survivor of Hurricane Katrina
I am my history
I am my Blackness
I am Black Power
I am Black Pride
I am each one teach one
I am unity makes a difference
I am it takes a village to raise a child
I am the falling tears of generations past
I am my journey
I am my history
I am my past
I am my Blackness
I am who I am
I am a Negro
I am colored
I am African-American
I am Black
I am my Blackness

www.ingramcontent.com/pod-product-compliance
Lightning Source LLC
Chambersburg PA
CBHW031246290426
44109CB00012B/459